P9-AQK-273

"How would you describe your faith? Strong? Bold? Consistent? Mature? If you are like so many fellow Christians, those are words you *wish* were synonymous with your walk with the Lord but sadly, they aren't. Why not? Step into the pages of this timely and important book to discover the potential each of us has to grow our faith. Learn to identify those stumbling blocks that get in the way of our being 'built up in him and established in the faith' (Colossians 2:7 ESV). The days of wimpy, tepid Christianity are over. Discover how to grow up in him, get grounded in his Word, and impact the world for Christ because small things really can become big!"

Janet Parshall, nationally syndicated talk show host

"Mike Novotny is one of those rare writers who is a real joy to read, and his new book, *What's Big Starts Small*, is no exception. In a world filled with shallow, 'positive-thinking' Christian books, Mike isn't afraid to tackle hard topics like pain, pride, worry, want, and having to wait. If you've ever struggled with your Christian life or been frustrated with God, this is the book for you. It's a close-up look at the threats we all face as believers and a road map to discovering our real potential."

Phil Cooke, PhD, media producer and author
of *The Way Back: How Christians Blew
Our Credibility and How We Get It Back*

"Mike Novotny's humor and honesty challenged me to look at the condition of my spiritual life, consider my priorities, and pray for greater usefulness. This book will help you see how to take the next step in your Christian walk."

Steve Hiller, network cohost of *Dawn and Steve
in the Morning*

"Our justification is perfect and pure. Our Christian life in response is full of mess. How can Christians keep moving forward instead of grinding to a halt in despair and confusion? Pastor Mike takes us on the faith-life journey with humor, honesty, transparency, and wit. You will enjoy the ride!"

Pastor Mark Jeske, former lead speaker of Time of Grace

"Pastor Mike has a truly remarkable ability to teach familiar Scripture in a fresh, eye-opening, exciting way! This book is spiritually meaty while at the same time funny, relevant, easy to read, and ultra-practical. I'm SO excited for how this book will make your faith come alive and grow deeper!"

Diana Kerr, certified professional life coach for overwhelmed, go-getter Christian women

"Mike Novotny has a winsome way of pointing us to the Truth that can develop giant faith from a tiny speck. Readable and engaging, What's Big Starts Small is a difference-maker!"

Dawn Rae, network cohost of Dawn and Steve in the Morning

"Those who have read Pastor Novotny's devotions or heard him preach on Time of Grace will find his new book, What's Big Starts Small, very helpful for their spiritual lives. His insights about Jesus' parable of the sower are perceptive and practical. Readers will gain a whole new appreciation for Jesus' message."

Donald Zietlow, President and CEO of Kwik Trip, Inc.

WHAT'S
BIG
STARTS
SMALL

Books by Mike Novotny

3 Words That Will Change Your Life

Gay & God: Loving Everyone God Made and Everything God Wrote

From Dirty to Dancing: God's Grace for Those Struggling with Pornography

Sexpectations: The Word Says It All

GOD Is Here: A Prayer Journal

No Fear Year: How to Live with Hope in a Broken World

The Impossible Made Possible: An Interactive Devotional Journey Toward Radical Forgiveness

How to Heal

What's Big Starts Small

WHAT'S BIG STARTS SMALL

6 WAYS TO GROW GREAT FAITH

MIKE NOVOTNY

BETHANYHOUSE

a division of Baker Publishing Group
Minneapolis, Minnesota

© 2022 by Time of Grace Ministry

Published by Bethany House Publishers
11400 Hampshire Avenue South
Minneapolis, Minnesota 55438
www.bethanyhouse.com

Bethany House Publishers is a division of
Baker Publishing Group, Grand Rapids, Michigan

Printed in the United States of America

All rights reserved. No part of this publication may be reproduced, stored in a retrieval system, or transmitted in any form or by any means—for example, electronic, photocopy, recording—without the prior written permission of the publisher. The only exception is brief quotations in printed reviews.

Library of Congress Cataloging-in-Publication Data
Names: Novotny, Mike, author.
Title: What's big starts small : 6 ways to grow great faith / Mike Novotny.
Description: Minneapolis, Minnesota : Bethany House Publishers, a division of
    Baker Publishing Group, [2022] | Includes bibliographical references.
Identifiers: LCCN 2022002387 | ISBN 9780764240034 (paperback) |
    ISBN 9780764240706 (casebound) | ISBN 9781493437412 (ebook)
Subjects: LCSH: Spiritual formation. | Sower (Parable)
Classification: LCC BV4511 .N75 2022 | DDC 248.4—dc23/eng/20220216
LC record available at https://lccn.loc.gov/2022002387

Unless otherwise indicated, Scripture quotations are from THE HOLY BIBLE, NEW INTERNATIONAL VERSION®, NIV® Copyright © 1973, 1978, 1984, 2011 by Biblica, Inc.® Used by permission. All rights reserved worldwide.

Scripture quotation marked ESV is taken from The Holy Bible, English Standard Version® (ESV®), copyright © 2001 by Crossway, a publishing ministry of Good News Publishers. Used by permission. All rights reserved. ESV Text Edition: 2016

Scripture quotation marked *The Message* is taken from *THE MESSAGE*, copyright © 1993, 2002, 2018 by Eugene H. Peterson. Used by permission of NavPress. All rights reserved. Represented by Tyndale House Publishers, Inc.

Cover design by Dan Pitts
Illustrators: Jason Jaspersen and Bethany Vredeveld

Author represented by Jason Jones

Baker Publishing Group publications use paper produced from sustainable forestry practices and post-consumer waste whenever possible.

22   23   24   25   26   27   28   7   6   5   4   3   2   1

To Mom
Without the seed you planted in my heart as a child,
this book (and so much more) might not exist.

Love,
Your son*

---

* I was going to write "your favorite son" just to make my brother mad, but I knew you wouldn't like that.

CONTENTS

PART 1

YOUR POTENTIAL AND JESUS' PARABLE

1

Exponential Potential

Up to Your Potential?

If you are reading this book,* I assume you have something in common with me: in the past year, you heard God's Word. You went to church, read devotions at home, podcasted sermons, listened to Christian radio, or scrolled through Bible passage posts on social media. You might even be one of those rare people who did all the things on that list. In fact, you might be the rarest of Christians who does all those things every week!

If that assumption is correct, let me make a second assumption about you—I bet that you, like me, wonder why your faith isn't all that great. I'm not talking about perfect faith—you are a saved sinner and not our sinless Savior, after all. I'm talking about great faith. Strong faith. Mature faith. The kind of faith that people notice and thank God for (Matthew 5:16). The faith that produces a pure life that wins over your non-Christian friends and family, not with your evangelistic words but with your extraordinary actions (1 Peter 3:1–2). The faith that gushes

---

* If you are *not* reading this book, I find it confusing how you made it to this footnote.

so much love that outsiders know that you must be a follower of Jesus (John 13:35).

I'm talking about the great faith that has no place for shame, self-loathing, or feeling alone since it trusts that God is for you, in you, and with you (Romans 8:31). Great faith that knows exactly what to do with a relapse, a spot of cancer, or a lifelong struggle with worry: run to the grace of your Savior, ask the Father for peace that goes beyond understanding, and rely on his Spirit to put sin to death (Romans 8:1–4). Great faith that casts all your anxiety on God because you have zero doubts that he cares for you (1 Peter 5:7). Great faith that believes that it is more blessed to give money than to receive it, no matter what tax bracket you are in (Acts 20:35). Great faith that preaches biblical truth at your own depressed heart and commands your feelings to submit to the facts of your salvation (Psalm 42:5). Great faith that trusts that the Bible's command about honoring your imperfect parents is not burdensome (1 John 5:3). Great faith that refuses to keep score in a relationship but instead makes you-first love its daily goal (1 Corinthians 13:5). Great faith that sees your children's tantrums as opportunities to make better disciples and not simply as annoyances that make Mommy angry (Ephesians 4:31–32). Great faith that sees God's face shining upon you despite all the messiness still within you (Numbers 6:25). In other words, faith that believes what God says and behaves accordingly.

Since "faith comes from hearing the message" (Romans 10:17), you would expect message hearers like us to have faith like this . . .

You got faith that great? (Just typing that last page made me feel un-great-er.)

So what happened? Why didn't the Word you heard seem to work? Why didn't "it is finished" finish your feelings of not being good enough for God? Why didn't Christ's "look at the birds" sermon keep you from looking at all the imaginary what-ifs you worry about? Why didn't the sermon series on spiritual priorities re-prioritize your schedule to seek God first? Why does your spiritual maturity seem stuck in puberty?

If your answer is, "Because I am a sinner living in this demonically deceived world," I would agree with everything except your logic. You are indeed a sinner who daily fights against your sinful nature (Galatians 5:17). And you are, lamentably, still in this world that tempts you in ten ways every two minutes (1 John 2:16). And the devil is still good at his job, lying with such subtlety that sin seems good in the moment (John 8:44).

But look back at your answer above. Your "because" lacks biblical logic, since it would disqualify any sinner from having great faith. But some Christians truly do have a more mature faith than others, proven by their ability to go through the same situations that we do yet respond in different ways. They battle the same flesh, live in the same world, and go to war against the same Satan, yet the outcome of their battles is notably different. Not perfect, but different.

I notice this difference all the time. Why was I the only person in the meeting who got defensive and made an honest discussion of an idea so unnecessarily awkward? Apparently, everyone else in the room found another path to take while I, prone as I am to wander, wandered away from humility and love. Why, on the soccer field, does my heart want me to be the best player instead of the best example of Christian love? Most of my teammates seem to handle defeat much better than I do, while I pout on the drive home and, the morning after, send an apologetic email for my sour attitude. Again.

Given my (1) occupation and (2) spiritual habits, you would assume I would be much better at these basic commandments. If I spent as much time with a guitar as I do with God, I would be a Gen X Jimi Hendrix. I read my Bible in the morning, podcast sermons while I shave, sing praises to Jesus while I drive to work, spend my entire workday with the Scriptures nearby (pastoral perk!), drive home with more podcasts, do a devotion with my family after dinner, and read Christian nonfiction until I turn out the lights.

Imagine if I spent an equal amount of time doing anything else. Block out that same time at the gym, and I would soon crush my current pull-up record.* If I immersed myself in an equivalent amount of Spanish, I would impress native speakers with my knowledge of the word for "pull-up."†

You get my point. On paper, I should be great at this Jesus thing, but *great* isn't a great word to describe my less-than-flattering faith. Am I just being too hard on myself? Is my faith actually growing but in slow, steady, hard-to-see ways? Or am I right to think that after all those church services and all those quiet times, I should have a lot more spiritual fruit by now?

Do you ever feel this way? If so, there is some news you need to hear.

Bad News/Good News/Great News

I have bad news: Jesus said that we often fall short of our potential because our souls are under an all-out assault by those who hate God. Even though we might hear the Word, we have spiritual enemies that appear before church, during our devotions, and after our amens. To quote Jesus, these villains

---

* One.
† *la dominada.* I had to Google that one, since I'm not great at Spanish or pull-ups.

attempt to "trample on," "snatch up," "wither," "scorch," and "choke out" God's truth before it does anything great in our lives.

In other words, counting your hours of hearing the Word to determine the greatness of your faith is no more accurate than counting the tomato seeds you spill in a parking lot to estimate how many ripe tomatoes you'll get. Great faith doesn't come from simply hearing the Word. It comes from planting the Word *and then* protecting it from its most common predators. To paraphrase Jesus, exponential faith only happens if we hear the Word, understand the Word, accept the Word, retain the Word, and persevere with the Word.

I have good news: Jesus told us the six specific ways that these enemies work, namely, through pride, pain, worries, wealth, wants, and not waiting. Our Savior, in love, snuck their playbook into one of his parables, affording us an incredible advantage to win more spiritual battles than ever before. Imagine if you were an NFL coach and somehow knew the play that your opponent was about to run. You would pay close attention and adjust accordingly because knowing your enemy's tactics is a key to victory.

I have great news: God wants to help you. The God of power and love wants his Word to reach its potential in you and through you. As you read his Book, God will forgive you for falling short, end your "I can't do this" pity party, and pick you up by his Spirit so that you can grow in faith, know Jesus even better, and love like never before. God *wants* that! Ponder that for a moment—God *wants* you to have great faith.

How do I know? Because every farmer wants fruit.

In the story we are about to study, Jesus compared our Father to a farmer. I've never met a farmer who simply wanted to get rid of seed without any desire for a future harvest. And I have yet to meet a God who simply wanted to get rid of his Word without any desire for a better you.

"Just go to church and get it over with," God never once said.

"Check that 'quiet-time' box and get on with your day," Jesus never once commanded.

"Just double-speed that worthless devotion," the Spirit never once encouraged.

God wants his Word to work wonders in your life. That is the entire reason he brought you into contact with the Bible. Church services, worship playlists, and home devotions have never been the end game for God, because this Farmer is after fruit. Lots of it.

A more loving, joyful, peaceful, patient, good, gentle, kind, faithful, and self-controlled you is what God wants (Galatians 5:22–23). A new you who can cast all your nighttime anxiety on him, be self-controlled in the face of clickbait news, and be content even when criticized is what God wants (1 Peter 5:7; Philippians 4:13). God wants to help you forgive what you can't forget about your father, to let go of what you can't control about your kids, and to know he delights in you even when you are postpartum depressed or despairing over your own sinfulness. Your growth is on the top of God's to-do list.

Meditate on that when you find your seat next Sunday in church or when you listen to that Christian audiobook during your morning workout. The God who controls all things has brought you—out of all the billions of people on the planet—into contact with this particular passage—out of the tens of thousands of options—for one specific purpose: spiritual growth.

"How much growth?" you ask.

More than you imagine.

Your Exponential Potential

During a chilly February in the early '80s, I was conceived. Since we are just beginning our writer-reader relationship, I will spare you the details, but, according to the science, my microscopic beginning created a six-foot, two-inch man who can dunk on a ten-foot rim.*

Isn't that insane? If my calculations are correct, my mother's egg grew 20,000 times its original size, an organic absurdity that is true, give or take a few inches, for billions of humans. Even LeBron James came from two things you could barely see!†

If you didn't know the science behind human development, would you ever believe the exponential growth that the average adult experiences? *Exponential* might sound like clickbait marketing jargon, but what other word fits a 20,000-times return on investment?

The same thing that happens with humans takes place in the garden. You would need an oversized laundry basket to carry the tomatoes that came from a seed as small as the "D" engraved on an average dime.

If you hadn't planted, watered, and witnessed it, wouldn't you dismiss it as fake news? But you do believe it because you have tasted and seen the potential that God has placed in small things.

Which brings me to the point of this book: according to Jesus, God's Word is like a seed.

Read those last six words one more time. If you have never trembled when you held the Bible in your hands or felt that nervous energy as you waited for church to begin, you might

---

* Dunk a tennis ball, that is. I once dunked a volleyball in the early 2000s as well. Please hold your applause.
† I've heard, just like me, LeBron can dunk a tennis ball too.

have missed the glorious truth that Jesus taught—God's Word is like a seed.

The Word seems so small—just a single verse from a single chapter in a single book on a single shelf; just another Sunday with another service that contains another message and another set of songs; just a verse of the day that the Bible App pushes to your phone; just a sermon podcast you listen to on 1.25 speed as you fold laundry or drive to the office.

But Jesus rejects "just a" thinking because he says that God's Word is like a seed. He refuses to scoff at our spiritual habits, no matter how insignificant they might seem to the world, because he has seen, throughout history, what the Word can produce in hearts like yours.

"Faith comes from hearing the message" (Romans 10:17).

"The words I have spoken to you—they are full of the Spirit and life" (John 6:63).

"But the seed falling on good soil . . . produces a crop, yielding a hundred, sixty or thirty times what was sown" (Matthew 13:23).

This is the exponential potential of the seed we call God's Word. And I have the harvest to prove it.

"Tell Me about Your Life Verse."

To verify Jesus' point, I emailed the staff at our church and asked each of them to tell me about his or her "life verse."

If you're not familiar with the church slang, a "life verse" is a Bible passage that, for whatever reason, becomes your go-to source for guidance, comfort, and strength. Even though there are over 31,000 verses in the Bible, a life verse is disproportionately important, a frequent guest that shows up in your thoughts, making bad days bearable and good days even better.

"Tell me about your life verse," I asked our staff, and the replies dinged into my inbox every hour:

One woman replied, "My go-to passage for many, many years has been, 'Trust in the LORD with all your heart and lean not on your own understanding' (Proverbs 3:5). That passage got me through many deaths in our immediate family and my husband losing his job."

A younger colleague shared, "'Do not fear, for I have redeemed you; I have summoned you by name; you are mine' (Isaiah 43:1). Being someone who battles anxiety, I find an example of pure love in this passage. These words remind me that God isn't saying, 'I guess I will take him' but instead that he has a desire that burns so greatly for me, even though I don't deserve it."

One parent on our staff explained why she adored Romans 15:13*—"Our three-year-old daughter was diagnosed with a brain tumor. As she was being treated through chemo and radiation, we did not know how her journey would go. Could I have joy and peace even going through this? Yes, because I know the GOD of hope. No matter what would happen during her struggle or our struggle here on earth, we have the HOPE of the resurrection by the power of the Holy Spirit."

A newer member on staff wrote, "When I'm outside in God's creation, this passage often comes to mind and puts my perspective back where it needs to be—'And these are but the outer fringe of his works; how faint the whisper we hear of him! Who then can understand the thunder of his power?' (Job 26:14). . . . The beauty around me, the love I feel for my husband, children, and my people, the work he gives me to do, the blessings too numerous for me to count are all just the faint whisper of what God is and what is to come."

What do all these stories have in common? They prove the exponential power of the Word of God. A single verse, sometimes even half a passage, can calm you when you feel anxious,

---

* "May the God of hope fill you with all joy and peace as you trust in him, so that you may overflow with hope by the power of the Holy Spirit."

open your eyes to the Creator's glory, and hold on to you as you let your little girl go into the arms of God.

You don't need to memorize the whole Book to be blessed. Sometimes it just takes a single word.

Please let that truth settle somewhere deep within you. According to Jesus, next Sunday could be *the* Sunday, the epic Sunday when you hear that one verse that grows and matures and blossoms into a laundry basket full of strength that will get you through your struggles with dating. Tomorrow morning could be *the* morning, the one when you open your Bible to "just a" random page and fix your thoughts on a truth that will finally inspire you to forgive your ex, love your exhausting sister, or leave the shame of your abortion at the foot of the cross.

You don't need a pilgrimage to Israel or a PhD in theology. You just need a Word as small as a seed.

The Big Picture

In the pages to come, we are going to unpack one of the most impactful stories that Jesus ever told, the parable of the sower.

In part 1 of this book, you will read our Savior's words and, I pray, meditate deeply upon them, asking the Holy Spirit to give you wisdom to understand them and power to put them into practice. Most of this book contains the words that I wrote, but this section is focused on the exact words that Jesus said. Read accordingly.

In part 2, we will examine the six threats to your potential as a hearer of God's Word. It won't always be comfortable, but I promise to tell you the truth, warn you of pitfalls you will likely fall into these days, and bring you back to the grace of Jesus in every single chapter. After all, even apostles like Paul knew how desperately they needed God's mercy (Romans 7:24–25).

In part 3, we will study what it means to have a soul that is "good soil," that is, a life that produces all that God intends for us when we hear his Word.

My prayer, even as I write these words, is that something in this book—a single chapter, a particular passage, a specific threat—would land in your heart like a seed and, in time, grow into something big, something that looks like great faith.

This Book (Kind of) Changed Me

I probably shouldn't tell you this, but Christian books like this one often overpromise in their introductions. "After reading this book, you will . . ." "When we are done, I promise that . . ." We authors love to guarantee results, since we know that results are what readers really want. No one wants to spend a few dollars and waste a few hours on something that doesn't work.

You are no fool to be skeptical about such promises. Perhaps you have heard them before in the dozens of Christian "change your life" books that did not quite change your life. Will this be another failed experiment in your desperate search for greater faith?

It struck me yesterday as I edited this book that my own story could serve as a test case. Since I typed the first draft of this book, ten months have passed, meaning that I have had nearly a year of following Jesus with these ideas in the front of my mind.

So did they change me? Did any of the biblical truths or practical tips in the pages to come make a difference in my day-to-day? Did this small book turn into something big for my faith?

Kind of. (How's that for a promise to keep you turning these pages?)

In chapter 10, I will share what changed in my spiritual life and what didn't. Sadly, I too quickly forgot some of Jesus' words once the first draft was done, leaving me in the same not-so-great place that I was before. I wish I could go back and tell myself to practice what I preached, since those who hear the Word and put it into practice are truly blessed (Matthew 7:24).

But, by God's grace, I did see some changes. I can't wait to tell you what happened with my prayer life and my relationship with screens after authoring this book.

But before we get there, we need to start with a story, a story Jesus told about a sower, his seeds, and a few soils, a story packed with meaning for your very soul.

Ever heard it?

STUDY QUESTIONS

1. Which part of your spiritual life would you love to see grow in exponential ways? What would be different if, one year from now, the Holy Spirit produced more fruit in you than ever before?

2. Given that our growth in this life will always fall short of God's ideal, why will it be essential for us to frequently come back to God's grace, Jesus' cross, and the fact that we are saved by the Lord's great faithfulness and not by our own great faith?

3. Can you think of a verse from the Bible (or a truth about what God is like) that has had an exponential impact on your life? How did you discover that verse/ truth? In what ways has it changed your life for the better?

4. Meditate on the following verses, jotting down some of the blessings that can come through God's Word—1 Peter 1:22–25; James 1:18–25; 2 Timothy 3:14–17.

5. Evaluate this statement: The devil loves it when people assume that simply hearing God's Word is the key to great faith.

6. Challenge: Text a few Christian friends and ask them if they have a life verse. What do their answers tell you about the potential of God's Word?

2

Seeds, Soils, and Souls

Jesus revealed the biggest threats to your God-given potential in one of his greatest stories.

If you've ever read Matthew, Mark, or Luke, three of the New Testament biographies of Jesus, you know that our Savior was a storyteller. He loved captivating the crowds with his tales of a son who defiantly ran away from home, a lone sheep that got separated from the flock, and two guys who walked into a church.*

These stories were officially called "parables," based on a Greek compound word (*pará* + *bállo*) that means to place something next to something else (think of how a "para-llel" line is placed next to another line). In his parables, Jesus would place his fictional story next to a nonfictional reality, a clever way to communicate truths about invisible spiritual things.

Throughout the gospels, Jesus told around 30 different parables. No single gospel contains all of them, but there are five specific parables that do appear in three of them (perhaps a Holy Spirit hint that they contain something God really doesn't

---

* That's not one of my lame attempts at humor but one of Jesus' best stories about salvation from Luke 18:9–14.

want us to miss!). Out of those five parables, one of them gets the most space on the sacred pages—the parable of the sower.

That extra biblical space was anything but a waste. In this short story, Jesus answers some of our most urgent questions— What does God want for me? Can his Word actually change me? If so, why isn't his Word changing me? How can I mature in my faith if I am still stuck in this world?

We will spend the entirety of this book examining this particular parable, so I'm going to ask you to do something that I never, ever do when I'm reading a book—slow down and think. I'm asking you to put the page-turning addict within you on a time-out and meditatively read Jesus' story in all three versions, circling words that jump off the page and jotting your questions and insights in the margins. Look for details that differ from one version of the parable to another, asking yourself what those words or phrases add to the story's meaning. Offer your best interpretation of what Jesus meant and why he wants you to hear this story today. Take at least 30 minutes (start a timer if you're the wiggly type) and ponder this essential lesson from Jesus' teaching.

Why take so much time when you could start reading part 2 ten minutes from now? I will let the author of Psalm 1 answer— "Blessed is the one . . . whose delight is in the law of the Lord, and who meditates on his law day and night. That person is like a tree planted by streams of water, which yields its fruit in season and whose leaf does not wither—whatever they do prospers" (verses 1–3). Do you long to prosper spiritually? Do you want your faith to be strong and fruitful? Then don't just read the law of the Lord. Meditate on it. Chew on it a bit. Interrogate it. Pray over it, asking the Holy Spirit to help you understand every word (he himself inspired it, after all!).

Personally, I would totally ignore those last two paragraphs and plow through to the next chapter. I'm sassy that way.* But

---

* Another example of my sassiness is turning the tub handle to "C" while my wife is showering. #husbandprank

you're smarter than I am. Take a deep breath, come back tomorrow if you need to, and let your soul soak in the words that God repeated for a good reason: because this is the story that can help you overcome the six threats to your exponential potential.

Matthew 13:1–9	Mark 4:1–8	Luke 8:4–8
That same day Jesus went out of the house and sat by the lake. Such large crowds gathered around him that he got into a boat and sat in it, while all the people stood on the shore. Then he told them many things in parables, saying: "A farmer went out to sow his seed. As he was scattering the seed, some fell along the path, and the birds came and ate it up. Some fell on rocky places, where it did not have much soil. It sprang up quickly, because the soil was shallow. But when the sun came up, the plants were scorched, and they withered because they had no root. Other seed fell among thorns, which grew up and choked the plants. Still other seed fell on good soil, where it produced a crop—a hundred, sixty or thirty times what was sown. Whoever has ears, let them hear."	Again Jesus began to teach by the lake. The crowd that gathered around him was so large that he got into a boat and sat in it out on the lake, while all the people were along the shore at the water's edge. He taught them many things by parables, and in his teaching said: "Listen! A farmer went out to sow his seed. As he was scattering the seed, some fell along the path, and the birds came and ate it up. Some fell on rocky places, where it did not have much soil. It sprang up quickly, because the soil was shallow. But when the sun came up, the plants were scorched, and they withered because they had no root. Other seed fell among thorns, which grew up and choked the plants, so that they did not bear grain. Still other seed fell on good soil. It came up, grew and produced a crop, some multiplying thirty, some sixty, some a hundred times."	While a large crowd was gathering and people were coming to Jesus from town after town, he told this parable: "A farmer went out to sow his seed. As he was scattering the seed, some fell along the path; it was trampled on, and the birds ate it up. Some fell on rocky ground, and when it came up, the plants withered because they had no moisture. Other seed fell among thorns, which grew up with it and choked the plants. Still other seed fell on good soil. It came up and yielded a crop, a hundred times more than was sown." When he said this, he called out, "Whoever has ears to hear, let them hear."

29

After reading this the first time, I notice . . .

After rereading Jesus' words, I also notice . . .

After reading Jesus' words for the third time, what catches my attention is . . .

What details differ from one version of the parable to another? What do those words or phrases add to the story's meaning?

What do you think Jesus meant by this parable? Why do you think he wants you to hear this story today?

Thankfully, this parable is one of the very few that Jesus immediately explained, like an answer key in the back of a high school geometry book. So if you are willing to slow down one more time, Jesus would love to let you in on the secrets of the kingdom of God.

You won't regret giving the next half hour of your life to the words that will protect the seed of God's Word until it can produce in you all that our Father intends.

Not sure if another extended time of meditation is worth your time? Maybe this picture, based on Psalm 1, will convince you to slow down and soak in God's truth.

Those who don't meditate . . . and those who do.

Matthew 13:18–23	Mark 4:14–20	Luke 8:11–15
Listen then to what the parable of the sower means: When anyone hears the message about the kingdom and does not understand it, the evil one comes and snatches away what was sown in their heart. This is the seed sown along the path. The seed falling on rocky ground refers to someone who hears the word and at once receives it with joy. But since they have no root, they last only a short time. When trouble or	The farmer sows the word. Some people are like seed along the path, where the word is sown. As soon as they hear it, Satan comes and takes away the word that was sown in them. Others, like seed sown on rocky places, hear the word and at once receive it with joy. But since they have no root, they last only a short time. When trouble or persecution comes because of the word, they quickly fall away. Still others,	This is the meaning of the parable: The seed is the word of God. Those along the path are the ones who hear, and then the devil comes and takes away the word from their hearts, so that they may not believe and be saved. Those on the rocky ground are the ones who receive the word with joy when they hear it, but they have no root. They believe for a while, but in the time of testing they fall away. The seed

persecution comes because of the word, they quickly fall away. The seed falling among the thorns refers to someone who hears the word, but the worries of this life and the deceitfulness of wealth choke the word, making it unfruitful. But the seed falling on good soil refers to someone who hears the word and understands it. This is the one who produces a crop, yielding a hundred, sixty or thirty times what was sown.

like seed sown among thorns, hear the word; but the worries of this life, the deceitfulness of wealth and the desires for other things come in and choke the word, making it unfruitful. Others, like seed sown on good soil, hear the word, accept it, and produce a crop—some thirty, some sixty, some a hundred times what was sown.

that fell among thorns stands for those who hear, but as they go on their way they are choked by life's worries, riches and pleasures, and they do not mature. But the seed on good soil stands for those with a noble and good heart, who hear the word, retain it, and by persevering produce a crop.

After reading this the first time, I notice . . .

After rereading Jesus' words, I also notice . . .

After reading Jesus' words for the third time, what catches my attention is . . .

What details differ from one version of the parable to another? What do those words or phrases add to the story's meaning?

_____

_____

_____

What do you think Jesus meant by this parable? Why do you think he wants you to hear this story today?

_____

_____

Do you get it? Did you catch the potential contained inside the seed of God's Word? And the various enemies that threaten to trample, snatch up, devour, scorch, and choke out the truth? And the harvest that could happen if only God would enable you to hear, understand, accept, retain, and persevere?

In the chapters that follow, we will explore each of the six threats that appear in this story, offering practical solutions to overcome each one and protect our interactions with the Word of God. So if you're ready to go deep, let's dig into the soil of Jesus' story and ask the Spirit to help us become the kind of Christians who bring back a hundred times what was sown into their hearts.

> Whoever has ears to hear, let them hear.
>
> Luke 8:8

PART 2

THE 6 THREATS

3

Pride

A farmer went out to sow his seed. As he was scattering the seed, some fell along the path; it was trampled on, and the birds ate it up. . . . When anyone hears the message about the kingdom and does not understand it, the evil one comes and snatches away what was sown in their heart . . . so that they may not believe and be saved. . . . This is the seed sown along the path.

Matthew 13; Luke 8, selected verses

A Misunderstanding about Misunderstanding

I almost wrote an entire book about something that Jesus didn't say.

One of my pastoral passions is helping people understand exactly what the Bible means. I am convinced that we too often pray "hallowed be your name" without the slightest idea what *hallowed* even is. We love the chorus "I'll worship your holy name" and the classic line "'Twas grace that taught my heart to fear," but how many of us could accurately explain what it means to worship a name or the theological connection between grace and fear?

Those common misunderstandings get in the way of worship since you can't enjoy or apply what you don't understand.

So when I read Jesus' parable, I latched on to these words— "When anyone hears the message about the kingdom *and does not understand it*, the evil one comes and snatches away what was sown in their heart" (Matthew 13:19).

Aha! Jesus must share my passion, because he lists "does not understand it" as the #1 threat to the potential of his Word. He even points a finger at the devil, accusing him of stuffing his beak full of seeds while God's family remains clueless and fruitless.

With Jesus' warning in mind, I went to work on a brand-new book about the importance of truly understanding the key words that God puts in his Word. The publisher even came up with a catchy title—*10 Words You Thought You Understood about God*.

But, in an ironic twist, I discovered that I had misunderstood Jesus' message about misunderstanding. The more I studied the parable of the sower, the more I realized that something more sinister was at play. The true threat was not an innocent "I don't understand what justification is" or pastors who use biblical jargon without defining their terms. The truth was darker, even demonic.

How did I come to this conclusion? I kept reading.

Soon after telling this parable, Jesus added,

In them is fulfilled the prophecy of Isaiah: "You will be ever hearing but never understanding. . . . For this people's heart has become calloused; they hardly hear with their ears, and they have closed their eyes. Otherwise they might see with their eyes, hear with their ears, understand with their hearts and turn, and I would heal them."

Matthew 13:14–15

Hmm. This didn't feel like an honest lack of knowledge. *Calloused* isn't the right word to describe a child who can't define *hallowed* or a first-time guest at church who thinks of *justified* as Justin Timberlake's first solo album.* Something more deliberate is happening here, an ignorance that is intentional. "They have closed their eyes."

In addition, Jesus quoted those words from the Old Testament prophet Isaiah. Isaiah's audience, who lived about seven hundred years before the Savior's birth, wasn't threatened by ignorance but rather by arrogance. They could "hardly hear with their ears" and often "closed their eyes," because they only opened their senses to prophets who tickled their ears with words they wanted to hear. Their hearts didn't understand, not because they couldn't but because they wouldn't.

They didn't want to.

What sealed the deal on my new understanding of this story was Jesus' choice of the word *trampled*, a violent verb devoid of innocence. That same word shows up in disturbing passages such as, "Do not give dogs what is sacred; do not throw your pearls to pigs. If you do, they may trample them under their feet, and turn and tear you to pieces" (Matthew 7:6). Even more graphically, the writer to the Hebrews used the word in his warning, "How much more severely do you think someone deserves to be punished who has trampled the Son of God underfoot, who has treated as an unholy thing the blood of the covenant that sanctified them, and who has insulted the Spirit of grace?" (Hebrews 10:29).

When I put together calloused hearts, an unwilling audience, and trampling feet, I realized that my initial interpretation didn't fit. Leave it to Jesus to mess with my book!

So what was Jesus talking about? He was talking about the first threat to the Bible's potential—Pride.

---

* If you didn't know that, this is a written warning that you need to prioritize some things in your life.

Pride refuses to understand what God says, not because it can't but because it won't.

It doesn't want to.

Do You Want To?

Is there anything in the Bible you don't want to understand?

That might seem like an odd question to ask the average reader of Christian nonfiction, but Jesus brought it up, so I'll be bold enough to ask it—Is there anything in Scripture that, honestly, your ears aren't open to hear?

If you walked into church and your pastor said, "I'd like to talk to you today about _____," is there any topic that, even if he was teaching out of an open Bible, would tempt you to tune out? Is there any doctrine that would cause you to cross your arms and mentally argue until the final amen?

For example, do you want to hear what the Bible says about loving people? The Bible has much to say about the people in your life, from your parents to your next-door neighbors, to your best friend, to the woman at work who is the exact opposite of you. In multiple places, the Scriptures give a game plan for how to treat friends, how often to forgive enemies, and what it looks like to love everyone. Would you like an in-depth study of 1 Corinthians 13, Philippians 2, Ephesians 4, and the book of 1 John so you can arrange your life accordingly, apologizing for pick-and-choose love and committing yourself publicly to imitating the unconditional love of Jesus?

Do you want to hear what the Bible says about money? Jesus was infatuated with money talk, packing his parables with lessons on generosity, warnings about wealth, and concern for the poor. Would you like to scrap your current budget and conform your finances to 1 Timothy 6, 2 Corinthians 8–9, and Luke 12, giving up the reasons why you can't give just yet and starting, perhaps for the first time, to offer your first and your best to God? Or, if you are a firstfruits giver, to push yourself to "excel in this grace of giving" as passionately as you try to grow in other areas of your spiritual life (2 Corinthians 8:7)?

Do you want to hear what the Bible says about sex, marriage, and divorce? Matthew 5, Matthew 19, 1 Corinthians 6–7, Genesis 2, and Ephesians 5 are a crash course on romance, roles in marriage, commitment, acceptable causes for divorce, singleness, and what types of sexual pleasure pass the test of purity. Would you like to understand all that God has to say about that so that you can embrace it personally and defend it publicly?

If something irks you about any of those questions, I would like you to pause, reread the previous paragraphs, and notice one thing—I barely said anything about anything. I never put a number on how many times you should forgive, gave an exact percentage of how much you should give, or listed the biblical causes for divorce. Instead, I just brought up the issues themselves.

So if you felt yourself growing moody, why was that?

If you ever feel your walls going up when your Father wants to talk, take note. The seed, with all its exponential potential, is in grave danger. The prince of pride is swooping down to snatch up the Word before it does a single thing, hoping you will ignore God's voice, close your ears, and reject the repentance that will bring you closer to the heart and mind of God.

To paraphrase Jesus, proud people have ears, but they don't have ears to hear.

Objections and Exceptions

There is a way to figure out if this type of pride is a threat to your faith—objections and exceptions. You find yourself rushing to the objections that make you the exception.

Take organized religion, for example. In both the Old and New Testaments, God organized religion, calling Christians to do life together under the authority of the spiritual leaders whom God has called to oversee their souls. "Have confidence in your leaders and submit to their authority, because they keep watch over you as those who must give an account" (Hebrews 13:17).

This passage says that you should (1) have spiritual leaders and (2) submit to your spiritual leaders because (3) those leaders must account for your soul before God. In other passages, such as 1 Timothy 3 and Titus 1, God demands a high level of character for those who desire to be pastors so that laziness, greed, and immorality don't sabotage the church's mission to make Jesus' name great.

If, however, you find your heart instantly rushing to objections that make you the exception, beware. "But I had a bad experience in the church." "But religion is filled with hypocrites." "But I know a pastor who was embezzling/abusing/having an affair." "But a building doesn't make you a good person." "But I still pray and connect with God when I'm out in nature."

Those statements might be true, but they don't undo the truth of Hebrews 13. And while I regret the negative experiences you have had with the church, Jesus didn't make a bad experience a good reason for DIY spirituality. He still wants you to live in an organized community. He still wants you, like me, to be pastored by a trained and qualified pastor. He still wants you to be in the habit of gathering around his Word with others. Despite being murdered by church leaders, Jesus still valued the church, as evidenced by a New Testament filled with letters to organized churches.

But pride offers an objection that makes you the exception.

Or consider the overwhelming number of Bible passages that speak about the poor. "But now as for what is inside you—be generous to the poor, and everything will be clean for you" (Luke 11:41). "But when you give a banquet, invite the poor" (Luke 14:13). "All they asked was that we should continue to remember the poor, the very thing I had been eager to do all along" (Galatians 2:10).

These passages reveal God's passion for those who lack the necessary resources to thrive in life. One of the defining characteristics of the early Christian church was a sacrificial willingness to provide for the poor, an attitude they learned from the prophets, the apostles, and from Christ himself.

But if you find your heart protecting your bank password and listing all the objections that make you the exception, beware. "But my taxes cover the poor." "But if they would just get a job and go to work . . ." "But I need to boost my college fund first . . ." "But if they have money for beer and cigarettes . . ." "But if I don't max out my investments now . . ." "But we really need new furniture . . ."

Those statements might contain bits of truth, but they don't negate the hundreds of seeds scattered in his Word about the way we should treat the poor. If you have a home (like I do), a garage (like I do), Netflix (like I do), video games (like I do), a closet that can barely contain your clothes (like I do), a savings account (like I do), then you are called to financially love the poor. You don't have to give a handout to every homeless person you see, but God is calling you to imitate his heart for the poor.

But pride offers an objection that makes you the exception.

Before you think that I am throwing stones, I confess that I face this threat too. For me, pride doesn't often trample on God's love for organized religion or Jesus' heart for the poor but rather on our Father's simple call to compassion: "When he saw the crowds, he had compassion on them, because they were harassed and helpless, like sheep without a shepherd" (Matthew 9:36). "Therefore, as God's chosen people, holy and dearly loved, clothe yourselves with compassion, kindness, humility, gentleness and patience" (Colossians 3:12). "Finally, all of you, be like-minded, be sympathetic, love one another, be compassionate and humble" (1 Peter 3:8).

These verses are an obvious call to selfless compassion, sacrificial humility, and Christ-like sympathy. In a world where so many people are hurting, limping through life with deep wounds, God wants his sons and daughters to slow down their busy schedules, set aside their to-do lists, and be clothed in daily compassion.

And I don't like that.

I am, by nature, a productive doer and not an instinctive feeler. Put me in a quiet office, and I will kill it for the glory of God—I read fast, write fast, and work fast. Put me in a crowded room of church members and guests, believers and skeptics, and you will witness a man who has his master's in mingling. But put me in a situation that requires compassion, less fixing and more feeling, fewer answers and more empathy, and I struggle. A lot.

Please don't misunderstand. I do love people, and I long to help people. But I prefer to help people in ways that are convenient for my personality. I want to serve God and shepherd his people well . . . just in ways that are easy for me. If hurting people would just (1) schedule their pain in my type-A weekly planner, (2) come to my office hoping for a list of applicable passages and helpful resources, and (3) move on as if I have fixed their problems in about an hour, I would love the call to compassion.

But compassion isn't like that.

There are moments when God is calling me to crumple up my plans, scrap my timetable, and weep with those who weep. Sometimes, like the good Samaritan, I come across a wounded soul when I am rushing to Jerusalem for an urgent meeting, yet God still commands compassion. Helping the hurting is not an interruption to the good work God has called me to do. It *is* the good work that God has called me to do.

Part of my heart—the ugly part I hate—wants to make an objection that allows me to be an exception. "But there are different gifts in the body of Christ, right, Father? Someone else is better at this than I am, and they could help in wonderful ways that I can't, right, God? And won't I do more good if I focus my time on the stuff I am gifted in and passionate about?"

I wonder if God just stares at the seed he sowed in my direction—"Be compassionate and humble."

But pride prevents what God intends. Before compassion produces a great harvest of love and healing, the enemy snatches up the Word and flies back up to his branch.

So while God has your attention, is there anything in his Word you don't want to understand?

I'll give you some space below to confess a few teachings that you honestly don't yet have ears to hear. Skim my previous examples and have the courage to admit the places you wish God would have said something else. You will never be able to defend yourself against this threat until you recognize it.

If I could edit the Bible, I would take out all the passages that command me to . . .

-

-

-

Why, Though?

Before we discover a way to overcome this threat, let's dig deeper and ask, *why?* Why would I be so reluctant to hear what God himself has to say? Why would you? He's God, after all.

The answer is . . . I.

Smack-dab in the middle of p-r-i-d-e is "I." God's Word, when clearly understood, often confronts "I"—what "I" want, what "I" prefer, how "I" like to do things. When Adam and Eve listened to the devil's lies, they noticed that the fruit was not only pleasing to the eyes but also pleasing to the "I."*

Consider how inconvenient God's commandments are to me, myself, and I:

- "Give to the poor." (But I *need* to save up for a new phone.)
- "Make every effort to keep the unity of the Spirit." (But I think she should apologize first.)
- "Let us not give up meeting together." (But I prefer to relax on my only day off.)
- "Love your enemies." (But I can't stand the thought of him.)
- "Husbands, love your wives like Christ loved the church." (But I haven't felt respected in a long time.)
- "Wives, submit to your husbands in everything." (But I have a better way to do things.)
- "Honor your father and mother." (But I am too busy to call my mom right now.)
- "Let no unwholesome talk come out of your mouth." (But I need to vent every now and then, you know?)

God calls us to deny the "I" and take up our crosses in love, but part of us will do anything to get out of it, even act like we don't understand. Pride laces up its treaded boots and tramples on any seed that threatens our comfortable status quo. And, with a grateful squawk, the devil lands on the firm path and enjoys another Scripture.

---

* You can't spell *lie* or *die* or *sin* without a center stage "I."

Back in college, I had a beloved/witty/wonderful/sarcastic/ devout professor whose memorable one-liners found their way into my long-term memory.* In reflecting on his own experiences in the church, he warned us about people who think, "Jesus loves me this I know . . . and this is all I want to know!"

I know Jesus loves me, and this is all I want to know. I know God is here with me and has a plan for me, but I don't want to know more. I want to understand that I'm bound for a better place, but I don't want to understand what the Bible says about *that*.

The question that confronts our pride every time we hear the Word is, "Do you want to understand?" When there's a will and a want, there is always a way.

So how do we overcome this threat so the seed of God's Word stands a chance?

I'm glad you asked.

An Answer to Pride

Protecting yourself against pride can be summarized in three short affirmations of faith:

God is good.
God knows better.
God wants what's best.

The proud part of our stubborn hearts needs to be beaten back with these three truths in order to soften the soil of our souls and give the seed a chance to become what God intends. Let's examine each one:

---

* Such as, "Smart answer, Mr. Novotny. I guess there's a first time for everything!"

God Is Good

There is an ancient scroll that I keep in my office. Its parchment is blackened from an encounter with fire—proof, perhaps, that it was snatched from the flames of hell itself.* Whatever its origins, the message on that scroll is, indeed, from the pit of darkness—God's Not Good.

This was the proud claim that the serpent peddled to Adam and Eve, the original lie that prevented God's creation from

reaching its exponential potential. They sided with a fallen angel and doubted their loving Father and, if their finger-pointing was any indication, would have continued blaming God and believing he wasn't good (Genesis 3:12).

However, God immediately debunked the accusation by making a promise that proved his goodness: "He will crush your head, and you will strike his heel" (Genesis 3:15).

Instead of leaving Adam and Eve ashamed and alone, fruitless and hopeless, God guaranteed that "he" would help. Even if it came at a great cost, the promised "he" would crush the devil's head.

This was the first promise of the "he" we know as Jesus, our ultimate proof that God is good. Whenever our pride questions the goodness of God and the wisdom of his plan for our lives, we bring ourselves back to the cross, the one place where pride's objections seem absurd.

There, on the cross, Jesus died for my "I," paid for your pride, and suffered for our sins in an epic effort to both save

---

* Okay, an artist from church actually made the scroll for me and "hell-ified" it with a lighter.

us and convince us that God is good. Despite the nails and the thorns and the shame, Jesus fixed his eyes on our forgiveness and refused to come down from the cross until he had proven that our God only wants what is best for us. Even though his holy face grimaced in pain and winced as the creation mocked their Creator, our Lord didn't give in—exhibit A in the interrogation of God's good nature. There, in an invisible trade, Jesus took away everything that would make God angry at us and replaced it with everything that would make God delighted in us, an exchange that many have called not just good but great. To the cruel soldiers, Jesus said, "Father, forgive them" (Luke 23:34). To a dying criminal, Jesus said, "You will be with me in paradise" (Luke 23:43). To a world that could never reach the finish line of holiness, Jesus said, "It is finished" (John 19:30).

He must be good!

Show me a God who only commands obedience, and I will question his goodness. But show me this God, a God who is willing to die for the godless, and my questions grow quiet. The enemy might whisper, "God's not good," but a Savior who dies for his enemies makes the lie too absurd to believe. A God who would give up everything for us must be good, good enough to trust.

> You see, at just the right time, when we were still powerless, Christ died for the ungodly. Very rarely will anyone die for a righteous person, though for a good person someone might possibly dare to die. But God demonstrates his own love for us in this: While we were still sinners, Christ died for us.
>
> Romans 5:6–8

This passage hangs, framed, in my kitchen, declaring to my family that Christ didn't die for the good and the worthy but for sinners, for the ungodly, for us. That is love. That is the proof that God is good.

My youngest daughter reminded me of this goodness the other day. On our better nights as a family, we take some quantity time to read God's Word, pray for each other, and sing a worship song together. After one such devotion, I asked my 11-year-old what song of praise she would like me to pull up on YouTube.

"That one, Daddy!" She pointed at the screen. So I clicked on "Goodness of God" and turned up the volume.* The worship leader sang about how God's goodness runs after us, the same truth that concludes Psalm 23.

"Daddy," my daughter explained once the song was over, "I was thinking about God's goodness." She put a hand, palm up, in front of me and used two fingers from her other hand to personify God's two-legged goodness, racing across her open palm, chasing my daughter down.

"His goodness runs after me. I can't get away from it!"

Well said, kiddo.

God's goodness chases us down. Like a good shepherd who can't stand the thought of losing a single sheep, God's goodness came after you when you were straying, endangered, and completely lost. Why? Because God is good.

And—here's my point—God doesn't stop being good when he speaks about that thing in the Bible you don't want to understand. He can't cease his goodness because he's God! By his very nature, "God is light; in him there is no darkness at all" (1 John 1:5). So despite your concerns, *that* word is a good word from a good God. Out of the overflow of God's heart, God speaks, which is why every word that comes from the mouth of the Lord must be good.

So perhaps you should take the truths that bother you to the foot of the cross—literally. Bring your Bible into a church or into a room in your home that has a cross, open it to that uncomfortable verse, and look up at the symbol of the goodness of

---

* Because hearing me sing is a true threat to anyone's enjoyment of worship.

God. Read aloud those words about kindness to your enemies, about submission to authorities, about whatever challenges your humility, allowing your eyes to bounce from the page to the place where Jesus humbled himself for you.

Speak truth to your reluctant heart, reminding it, "God is good. This teaching is hard, but God is good. This will change things for me, but God is good. He must be. He gave his only Son for me."

God Knows Better

Not only is God good; God also knows better.

The gap between God's knowledge and ours is greater than the size difference between an acorn and an oak tree. "As the heavens are higher than the earth, so are my ways higher than your ways and my thoughts than your thoughts" (Isaiah 55:9). That's God's way of saying that you can take a running start or jump off a stack of college textbooks, but your thoughts will never reach the heights of his knowledge and wisdom. While my pride would love to pat me on the back for my ACT score, I know .00000000001% of what there is to know, and even what I think I know is often mistaken.

That's why it's good for us to take a deep breath and admit that we are not God. While our pride persists in believing that our thoughts, our friends, our parents, our professors, our authors, our culture, our whoever is the source of truth, God knows better.

He is God, after all.

Thankfully, God is above and beyond cultural blind spots and personal biases. Western culture might idolize its independence, frantically clinging to "my truth," but God is not deceived by such idols. Eastern cultures might take the concept of honor too far, shaming sinners and disowning those who have dishonored the family name, but God is not bound by such boundaries. Modern Americans treasure being true to themselves without considering the complicated mess of desires that exists in their hearts, while earlier Americans clung to rigid gender stereotypes that demeaned women and excused men, but God's thoughts are infinitely higher than both.

God knows better.

Jesus' younger brother James picked up on the gardening metaphor and encouraged us, "Humbly accept the word planted in you" (James 1:21). God is not only good; he's good at being right. So humbly accept the words that he speaks.

Yes, some of Jesus' teachings will be scandalous (especially the stuff about unconditional love). Yes, most of the Spirit's inspired words will require self-denial and sacrificial service. But, yes, you can seek understanding without fear because God knows better.

Let God's knowledge rototill your proud heart. "Break up your unplowed ground; for it is time to seek the LORD, until he comes and showers his righteousness on you" (Hosea 10:12). Pride needs to be plowed up, its arrogant thoughts smashed like stubborn clumps of dirt so that God can shower his righteousness on you.

His heart has good intentions. You can trust him because he is holy. Because he is holy, he is always good.

Years ago, God proved his goodness when our church spent three weeks talking about America's least favorite word—*submit*.

When we hear the word *submission*, our minds envision a choke hold that forces an MMA fighter to tap out or a mousy wife caving in to her husband's ogreish desires for sex, steak, and more sex. I dare you to use the s-word in casual conversation and then snap a quick pic of your friends' instinctive reactions around the table.

It would be very tempting to skip those Scriptures, but God knows better.

Our church discovered that *submit* actually comes from two Latin words, *sub* and *mittere*. *Sub* means "under" (like a submarine goes "under" the water), and *mittere* means "to put/place." So *sub-mit* means "to put yourself under" another person, to put their will above yours. Or, as we simplified it, to submit means to say, "You first!"

That phrase became a seed in our community, something that has been growing ever since that series, a truth that has shaped our couples' counseling, instructed us how to live under flawed government leaders, and helped us navigate messy situations at work (1 Peter 2:13–3:7). Those two words turned into T-shirts, social media posts, and even a rhyme—"Me first makes a mess, but you first makes us blessed."

While submission itself is biblically connected to God-given authority, we started to see how God loves all our relationships to be filled with a "You first!" attitude, just as Jesus put us first when he gave up his will in the Garden of Gethsemane (Matthew 26:39). This is why my wife, Kim, and I constantly tell our daughters about the power of "You first!" and why every volunteer at our church puts on a "You First" shirt before showing up to serve.

An entire series on a cringe-worthy word? It would have been very tempting to close our ears, harden our hearts, and move on to more socially acceptable Scriptures, but a good God knew better. He blessed us.

He always does.

God Wants What's Best

When I was two years old, I almost murdered my mother.

My parents had decided to move from the shores of Lake Michigan up to Green Bay, Wisconsin, a change that would take me away from one of my fellow diaper-wearing friends. According to my mother, I didn't take the decision very well, which is why I attempted to kill her.

She was driving us to our new home for the first time, crossing the massive bridge that spans the Fox River, when I used my toddler skills to unbuckle my car seat, stand up, and deliver a series of ham-fisted punches to the back of her head.*

Thankfully, Mom managed to keep the car from plunging into the cold waters below, and we both lived to tell the story. And, in time, I came to see that my parents were doing what was best for our family, even if I didn't quite grasp it at the time.

God is a lot like that.

He truly wants what is best for us. When he invites us along for the spiritual ride we call faith, he isn't trying to drive us into destruction or speed away from lasting happiness. Just the opposite. He, like the good Father he is, is taking us in the direction of long-term blessings, even if our pride can only see the short-term losses.

So when pride swears, "This is the worst!" we remember that our Father wants the best.

God doesn't want you to be part of an organized church community just to rob you of an hour each week and subject you to miserable religious experiences. No, he wants you to be watched over by a pastor who knows your name, encouraged by people who know your story, defended by friends who know your weaknesses, refined by doing life with in-progress people, and structured so that you don't stray from what is healthy and good.

Nor is God encouraging my compassion just to mess with my schedule. Rather, he knows how mutually beneficial it is for me to feel the pain of the people whom I pastor, how my

---

* If God were into karma, this incident would have left me with great cosmic debt.

presence in the midst of their pain provides comfort for them and wisdom for me. I am a better preacher and writer, less tempted by simplistic solutions and here-and-now answers, when I walk with my brothers and sisters through the valley of the shadow of death. Such conversations may challenge me in the moment, but they bless me in the marathon of life.

And God isn't commanding you to forgive your ex 77 straight times just to make you a miserable doormat. He wants to free you from the never-ending cycle of hurt, the toxic trap of bitter thoughts, and the foolish attempt to fix his wrongs with your wrongs. He knows that forgiveness is freedom, and he wants what's best.

Our Father only wants, in the end, what is best.

Those Who Humble Themselves . . .

In the modern town of Bethlehem, there is an ancient church built over the supposed spot where Jesus Christ was born. What is almost as interesting as the inside of that church, however, is the entrance to it.

The church entrance is called the Door of Humility, and most adult visitors have to lower themselves to pass through the four-foot, three-inch opening. For a guy like me, that is some significant bowing low!

But those who humble themselves are exalted. Once inside, you see one of the oldest standing Christian churches on earth, filled with ancient paintings of the Magi, the grotto of Jesus' birth, and a sense of transcendence that few spaces can match.

In many ways, that church is like our faith. God's truth is humbling, and our pride wants to rise up and shout truth down. But those who bow low, confessing that God is good, that God knows better, and that God wants what is best, are exalted.

So talk back to your pride today. Tell it that if Jesus was born to save you, then God must be good. If Jesus' hardest words come from the lips of the One who is "the Truth," then God must know better (John 14:6). And if Jesus would give his life for you despite your pride, then God must want what is best.

Fix your eyes on your merciful God. That's how you protect his Word from the threat of pride.

STUDY QUESTIONS

1. Which topics/teachings/doctrines most often get your guard up? Looking back at your personal story and looking around at our culture, why do you think you chose those specific topics instead of all the others?

2. The apostle Paul claimed, "The mind governed by the flesh is hostile to God; it does not submit to God's law, nor can it do so" (Romans 8:7). Why doesn't "the flesh" (the sinful part of your heart) want to submit to God's truth? How does your answer drive you to the Holy Spirit and his ability to change your heart?

3. Evaluate this statement: In a culture that constantly tells you to "live your truth," it is harder than ever for Christians to submit their opinions to God's Word. Explain your answer.

4. Second Corinthians 5 says, "If we are 'out of our mind,' as some say, it is for God; if we are in our right mind, it is for you. For Christ's love compels us, because we are convinced that one died for all, and therefore all died. And he died for all, that those who live should no longer live for themselves but for him who died for them and was raised again" (verses 13–15). In your own words, explain how the love of Christ connects to your desire to submit to God and live according to his Word.

5. Proverbs 3:5–7 says, "Trust in the LORD with all your heart and lean not on your own understanding; in all your ways submit to him, and he will make your paths straight. Do not be wise in your own eyes; fear the LORD and shun evil." Find at least three connections between these verses and the chapter you just read.

6. Challenge: Find a quiet time to sit in front of a cross. With eyes fixed on the symbol of your salvation, talk to God about the part of his Word that you don't want to understand. Ask him to overcome that pride with the assurance of his goodness, knowledge, and love.

4

Pain

Some [seed] fell on rocky places, where it did not have much soil. It sprang up quickly, because the soil was shallow. But when the sun came up, the plants were scorched, and they withered because they had no root/no moisture. . . . Those on the rocky ground are the ones who receive the word with joy when they hear it, but they have no root. They believe for a while, but in the time of testing they fall away. When trouble or persecution comes because of the word, they quickly fall away.

Matthew 13; Mark 4; Luke 8, selected verses

Sad Stories

I am a story sponge. As a guy who loves God, loves people, and loves bringing the two together, I soak in stories and then squeeze them out as a storyteller.

Every month, in fact, I gather as many stories as I can and, while respecting confidentiality, share them with as many people as I can, celebrating the work that the Spirit is doing through our ministry. God is reaching people, teaching people, and saving people, using our services, sermons, and personal conversations like seeds that burst open with their divine potential.

"I saw my friend's faith, and I needed to know more," a young man confessed when I met him in jail for the first time.

"That thing you said about unconditional love was incredible," a victim of childhood sex trafficking told me after joining us for church the previous Sunday.

"Can God forgive *that?*" a dead-serious military veteran asked after telling me what he had done decades earlier.

If stories came with nutrition facts, these would be packed with 100% of our daily inspiration, which is why I love to hear them, share them, and boast about the blessings that show up when God's Word is heard.

But there is a heartbreaking problem with being a storyteller—sometimes the stories don't end as well as they started. Sometimes the guy who said he was all in ends up, suddenly, entirely out. Sometimes the girl who loved to gather with God's people in her teens turns into a 20-something with a 52-week churchless streak. Sometimes the first seed to appear above the soil in the spring didn't survive the heat of summer to produce fruit in the fall.

Has this ever happened to you? While you were sitting in church, you could almost sense the Holy Spirit convicting you, comforting you, and strengthening you to take a next step, to leave old ways behind and embrace your new life in Christ. You said, "Amen!" and meant it.

But then you went back to college. Or back to work. Or back to your boyfriend. Or back to the real world. And, in the process, something changed. What happened?

Jesus knows, and he wants you to know too. It's the second threat to your God-given potential: pain. In particular, it is the pain of people pushing back against the truths of God's Word.

The Time of Testing

God's truth, depending on your audience, can turn into your personal time of testing. You can be as loving and patient and upright as Jesus himself, but trouble nevertheless will come, according to Jesus himself, "because of the word."

And that will be your test.

You might love the Word when your churchgoing friend shares the message of life through Jesus, but what happens when your other friends call your new views of salvation narrow, exclusive, and judgmental? The pastor might use the Word to forgive you when you feel ashamed or comfort you when you feel overwhelmed, but when you quote that same Word to tell your family that the objective truth about sexuality or politics or gender or justice is in the Word and not in their hearts, what then?

Truth will cause trouble.

If the first threat is the pride that comes from inside, this threat is the pain that comes from outside. Since the Word will confront the pride in others' hearts, their hearts might beat fast with defensiveness and have no desire to hear, learn, or understand.

A few weeks ago, a guy from our church told me about a recent experience he had with online dating. He had connected with a woman through a site and started a texting conversation to test the waters, and she soon wanted to talk about politics and social issues. In particular, she wanted to know his views on abortion.

By God's timing, I had just spent three entire weeks preaching on the topic, exploring the issue from every angle after some intense research and biblical study. I'm not sure if I succeeded or not, but I attempted to be balanced, compassionate, and respectful of all the issues that surround the moral, ethical, and legal dimensions of abortion.

So instead of texting a quick response to his online friend, this gentleman sent a link to the sermon series. "You should listen to this." To her credit, she did.

And then she was done. "If you don't acknowledge my autonomy," she soon replied, "then this won't work. Have a nice life."

Autonomy, the belief that we rule ourselves instead of being ruled by God, didn't fit in her worldview. So the basic message of God as our Creator, Father, and King caused trouble, so much trouble that she had no desire to learn more about Jesus or more about my friend.

"Trouble . . . comes because of the word."

If you have read any of the gospels, this fact should not rattle you. Jesus not only personally faced rejection but also frequently promised to pass it on to his friends. The night before he bled, Jesus followed up his teaching on the potential of their lives with a blunt reminder that the world would not applaud their spiritual growth.

> I chose you and appointed you so that you might go and bear fruit—fruit that will last—and so that whatever you ask in my name the Father will give you. This is my command: Love each other. If the world hates you, keep in mind that it hated me first.
>
> John 15:16–18

If that shocks you, open your Bible to John 15 and read the rest of the chapter where Jesus forecasts the blazing sun of persecution and hatred for both the Father and his faithful kids, which is what historically happened. If the traditions of the early church are true, then the men who were there that night fulfilled what Jesus predicted. They suffered and died for the sake of truth.

James? Beheaded. Peter? Crucified. Thomas? Run through with spears.

What did these guys do wrong? They believed and behaved like Jesus.

When you humble yourself and hear the Word, hallowing God's name, asking for the coming of God's kingdom, and praying for the doing of God's will, those who love God will love you and those who don't love God won't. You might not end up crucified like Peter, but you will feel the pain of being labeled by our culture, the sting of rejection from a former friend, and the loneliness of being the only one in the room who agrees with Jesus.

Are you prepared for such pain? I hope so, because your potential lives on the other side of pain.

So let's get practical by examining which biblical truths might cost you the approval of those you know and love. Ironically, it might be the truths you love the most that they cannot stand.

Seven Truths Christians Love (and Non-Christians Don't)

1a. God made you.

God made you in your mother's womb and, like a one-of-a-kind Picasso, that makes you priceless. Our world is quick to determine your worth based on your BMI or your GPA, but God has declared that you—yes, you!—matter more than you will ever know. You are not an accident or a meaningless blip in the history of the cosmos. You are his creation. You count. Because you are his.

> I praise you because I am fearfully and wonderfully made.
>
> Psalm 139:14

1b. If God made you, you are not your own.

God rightfully owns everything that he has made. That means that your Creator owns you, and any claim to autonomy is as laughable as a toddler who claims to own the house he lives in. Therefore, it is God's life, not your life; his body, not your body; his time, not your time. "The earth is the LORD's, and everything in it, the world, and all who live in it" (Psalm 24:1), which includes you and everything you thought was yours.

> You are not your own.
>
> 1 Corinthians 6:19

2a. God loves you.

If God loves the world, by simple logic God loves you. Just as Jesus didn't reserve his love for the VIPs and PhDs but invested in the average, the forgotten, and the common, God's heart still beats for people the world fails to notice. You don't have to be a varsity starter, a class president, a social influencer, or a parent-of-the-year to get God's love because love is just what God does. Love is just who God is.

> God so loved the world that he gave his one and only Son.
>
> John 3:16

2b. If God loves you, you must love them.

If God loved you when you were the least lovable, then imitating God means loving the least lovable too. Dismissing people or people groups is morally loathsome to love, even if those groups are registered sex offenders or passionate members of the political party you cannot stand.

> If you love those who love you, what reward will you get? Are not even the tax collectors doing that? And if you greet only your own people, what are you doing more than others? Do not even pagans do that? Be perfect, therefore, as your heavenly Father is perfect.
>
> Matthew 5:46–48

3a. God forgave you.

In a résumé-insisting culture, God stands apart. We are so used to contracts, wages, and getting what we pay for that the undeserved, unearned, freely given grace of God is almost too good to believe. We get out of financial debt by work. We fix broken marriages by work. We get scholarships and promotions by work. But God works apart from works. He just gives, forgives, and saves, not because of what you do but instead because of what Jesus has done.

> For it is by grace you have been saved, through faith—and this is not from yourselves, it is the gift of God—not by works, so that no one can boast.
>
> Ephesians 2:8–9

3b. If God forgave you, you must forgive them.

If Jesus didn't get revenge on you for your sins, then you cannot get revenge on them for theirs. Your ex-husband may be slandering you every chance he gets, but you cannot guiltlessly imitate his sin. Your online gaming rival may talk trash every time he is ahead, but you cannot rub it in his face when the tables turn. Your critics may be ripe for criticism, but you must take the high road.

You are forgiven. You must forgive.

> For if you forgive other people when they sin against you, your heavenly Father will also forgive you. But if you do not forgive others their sins, your Father will not forgive your sins.
>
> Matthew 6:14–15

4a. God conquered death for you.

God defeated the one enemy that we can't: death. Jesus walked into the grave, allowing his sacred life to be swallowed up by our undefeated enemy, and then, on the most glorious day in history, Jesus rose, changing death from champ into chump. Now, for everyone who trusts in the risen Christ, death has lost its sting and become a shadow we simply pass through. The unavoidable period to end our lives is now a comma that ushers us into unfathomable happiness.

> By his death he might break the power of him who holds the power of death—that is, the devil—and free those who all their lives were held in slavery by their fear of death.
>
> Hebrews 2:14–15

4b. If God conquered death for you, death can only be conquered through God.

The empty tomb is the echoing proof that we need Jesus. Death will defeat you without faith in Jesus as the defeater of death. Call him a prophet, a teacher, or a good man, and you will die forever. Deny his divinity, diminish his identity, and death will wrap its bony fingers around your soul.

> Jesus said to her, "I am the resurrection and the life. The one who believes in me will live, even though they die; and whoever lives by believing in me will never die. Do you believe this?"
>
> John 11:25–26

5a. God gives eternal life to you.

Nothing lasts forever. As much as we try to keep our bodies healthy, our friendships strong, and our dreams alive, even the best things eventually come to an end . . . except for life itself. Through the love, life, death, and resurrection of Jesus, God is offering us an eternal life, a never-ending eternity of comfort, safety, love, understanding, kindness, laughter, and amazement.

Compared to that eternity, everything you are going through is nothing. What seems like forever, in retrospect, will be the blink of an eye, a labor pain that passes by the end of the day and births happiness that words cannot describe.

> I consider that our present sufferings are not worth comparing with the glory that will be revealed in us.
>
> Romans 8:18

5b. If God gives eternal life to you, then eternal life can only be found through God.

It seems absurd to suggest that most people don't end up in a better place, but that is exactly what Jesus suggested. In fact, he declared it, describing the road to life as narrow compared to the superhighway to destruction (Matthew 7:14). Good intentions, above-average morality, and works-based religions are ten-foot ladders that cannot reach the heights of eternal life. Only Jesus can.

> Jesus answered, "I am the way and the truth and the life. No one comes to the Father except through me."
>
> John 14:6

6a. God speaks truth to troubled minds.

If your mind is anything like mine, you have a lot going on up there. The thoughts that fill my head are wild and unpredictable, one moment logical, the next conspiratorial. Especially when I am overwhelmed or anxious, my feelings couldn't care less about fact-checking themselves.

But God speaks truth. When you don't feel loved, God vetoes your feelings and speaks truth. When you are convinced God is still angry and isn't quite ready to forgive you, God bangs his gavel, points an authoritative finger at his Son, smiles, and speaks truth.

If our hearts condemn us, we know that God is greater than our hearts, and he knows everything.

1 John 3:20

6b. If God speaks truth to you, then "your truth" makes God laugh.

Perhaps the most hate-able thing about the Word is how little trust it puts in you. The prophets, the apostles, and Jesus himself call your heart "deceitful," your nature "deserving of wrath," and our very race "evil" (Jeremiah 17:9; Ephesians 2:3; Matthew 7:11). So when you claim to "speak your truth," God chuckles, wondering why you would ever assume that your feelings are anywhere close to the truth.

Truth, if dictionaries have any authority over our hearts, is defined as what is accurate, correct, and factual. Those objective adjectives are not within you but rather within him, and anyone who disagrees has been deceived. Jesus prayed to God (and not you), "Your word is truth" (John 17:17).

7a. God has a plan for you.

We can get through a lot if we know there is a reason. Teenagers can get through exams if they know graduation (or a generous scholarship) is on the line. Athletes can push themselves to near exhaustion in practice if it gives them a chance at a championship in the playoffs. And mothers can literally push a human out of their bodies just to have a baby!*

Christians believe that God always has a plan. Always. "There's a reason for everything" is not a foolish thing to believe, because God guarantees that he is working out all things for our good. Our mental health struggles. The frustrating decisions of our manager. The political changes in our nation. All

---

* Consider the physics of this the next time it is your birthday. Then buy your mom something nice.

things are under God's control, which means there is always a plan for those who love God.

> We know that in all things God works for the good of those who love him.
>
> Romans 8:28

7b. If God has a plan for you, then your plans are relatively unimportant.

Like me, you probably have a personal plan to stay healthy, moderately wealthy, and relatively happy. But those plans aren't anywhere close to what Jesus promised his closest friends. When he told them they would make a difference in the world, it mostly involved preaching the truth until people hated them enough to insult them, drive them out of town, or even kill them. Your bucket list has little support from the Bible. God has other plans to bring his kingdom to earth.

> If you belonged to the world, it would love you as its own. As it is, you do not belong to the world, but I have chosen you out of the world. That is why the world hates you.
>
> John 15:19

Ah!!! Can you imagine if this was the first time you had ever heard those seven statements? You are wonderfully made, divinely loved, completely forgiven, absolutely immortal, eternally secure, firmly held, and supernaturally safe through Jesus.

No wonder they call this the gospel. This is better news than an 18-wheeler full of Swedish Fish tipping over in your driveway!* This instantly evident good news explains why Jesus says that some people spring up quickly and receive the Word with joy.

---

* A request that has been on my prayer list for many, many years.

But truth is a troublemaker. Jesus says, "When trouble or persecution comes because of the word . . ." (Matthew 13:21). Sometimes the very words that seem wonderful to you sound miserable to them. And once "they" don't approve, your time of testing has come. Now you will have to choose—him or them. You won't be able to have both, and the pain of that choice threatens to overwhelm and outvote all that joy you used to feel.

As much as I love seeing someone on fire for the Word during their first few months at church, Jesus warns us about the initial excitement we feel: "They believe for a while, but in the time of testing they fall away" (Luke 8:13). Like a couple of teenagers who pass beyond their puppy love, some people lose their passion for Jesus. A new stage of the relationship arrives, one that challenges as often as it blesses, where we can't enjoy God's love and have the world's love too.

Why, Though?

Part of me wants to shrug and say, "So what? You can't make everyone happy, so who cares if people don't approve of what Jesus said? They are just people. They are average middle-school kids, run-of-the-mill neighbors, and a handful of the seven billion humans who will be dead and forgotten within a generation. They forget the passwords to their social media accounts and have empty Taco Bell wrappers under their car seats. Who cares if they don't like the truth?"

That's easy to say but so hard to believe, isn't it?

The truth is that I like being liked by people. I want to follow the Lord, but I want to be likeable while I do it. I want to be the exception to Jesus' prediction, finding some way to get God's approval and the world's applause at the same time. Maybe if I don't push my faith too fast . . . Maybe if I make sure to love people well . . . Maybe if I don't thump the Bible or cram it down anyone's throat . . . Maybe if I am cool with craft beer, have a tattoo, and dance at weddings . . . Maybe if I know their shows and can quote their songs . . . Maybe there's a way for the world to like me as I love God.

Our hearts long for belonging. Despite our initial joy in Jesus, we deeply want to be admired by our professors, invited to a coworker's party, and on the right side of history (as declared by those who claim to know what that side is). I'm honestly not that excited to be culturally canceled, quickly labeled, and lumped in with the Crusaders and racists who also claimed to be faithful to Jesus.

The sun in Jesus' story makes me sweat too, and I have a hunch that this threat also threatens you. Few of us are so confident in our God-given identity that we are unaffected by the reactions of those we respect.

Which is why we need to add soil to our shallow souls.

The Answer to Pain

To find Jesus' answer to the threat of pain, think about what causes plants to wither. According to the basics of photosynthesis, green things grow through soil, sun, and sufficient water, so when the rain is scarce and the sun is strong, plants rely on below-the-surface resources. Their roots reach down into the dirt, pulling up moisture to plump up the plant's cells and keep the plant green and growing.

This biology helps us figure out a solution to the world's rejection. To protect our joy, we need to tap into another source of life, one that exists deep below the surface. The roots of our faith need to stretch down into places the world can't see in order for the seed to survive. Jesus described some people like rocky places that "did not have much soil," implying that a shallow soul will dry up quickly, while a soul that has depth can withstand a drought of people's approval.

You might accuse me of a circular argument here, but it appears that the answer to giving up on God is getting more of God. We wither not primarily because of the Word but because we haven't grasped the Word. We have yet to arrive at the treasure that is found in the depths of Scripture, that is, the worthiness of God.

Teenagers push through long hours of studying for exams because they believe college is worth it. Marathoners keep running at mile 22 despite the agony because they believe the finish line is worth it. Couples have honest, painful conversations because they believe keeping their marriage together is worth it. And Christians hold on to Christ, despite the pain, when they believe that Jesus is worth it.

Just as there are three things to neutralize threat #1 (God is good, God knows better, God wants what's best), there are three simple truths to deal with the trouble that truth causes:

He > Them. His > Theirs. Then > Now.

He > Them

Here's a report from the Department of the Obvious: God is greater than people. The eternal God is greater than the kids on the bus, the boy you like, your favorite professor, and the folks in the comment section. I am not disparaging the people we know and love but simply reminding you of the infinite worth of the One whom you cannot see.

In speaking of God, Moses once gushed, "Who is like you—majestic in holiness, awesome in glory, working wonders?" (Exodus 15:11).

In speaking of people, Isaiah once commanded, "Stop trusting in mere humans, who have but a breath in their nostrils. Why hold them in esteem?" (Isaiah 2:22).

In those moments when worshiping God is costly, when the world shakes its head and scoffs at your biblical beliefs, let

Moses and Isaiah do the math for your people-pleasing heart—
God is greater! God is awesome in glory, while that guy has but
a breath in his nostrils.

If you can only make one of the two happy, remember that
God is worthy!

Let's make this practical. In the chart below, I'd love for you
to compare God to "them," to the people who are troubled by
the biblical truths that you believe. Take a moment to (1) fill in
all the things you know and love about God and (2) fill in all
the things you know and love about them. Finally, ask yourself
the honest question, *Who is greater?* by choosing > or < in the
center column.

God	> or < ?	Them
God is . . .		My parents are . . .
		My best friend is . . .
		My significant other is . . .
		My classmates/coworkers are . . .
		My teachers/professors are . . .
		My _____ is . . .

So did you end up agreeing with Moses and Isaiah? If you can't make him and them happy, remind your heart that God is greater.

His > Theirs

Not only is God greater than them; his blessing is greater than theirs.

If you give up on God, you'll get your friends' love, applause, and approval, but those fickle blessings won't bless you for long. But if you hold on to God, retaining his Word and persevering despite the pain, you will end up with blessings that do not end.

This is what Peter held on to when the crowds scoffed at anyone who would believe the absurd teachings of Jesus. A stadium of fans had gathered on the day when the Lord fed the five thousand, but once Jesus stopped providing and started preaching, the fans flooded out the door.

"'You do not want to leave too, do you?' Jesus asked the Twelve," the question upon which all their spiritual potential was hanging. "Simon Peter answered him, 'Lord, to whom shall we go? You have the words of eternal life. We have come to believe and to know that you are the Holy One of God'" (John 6:67–69).

Not only does Peter point out that He > Them ("you are the Holy One of God"); he also mentions that His > Theirs. "Jesus, you have the words of eternal life. Who else can bless me with a free pass to spend forever with God? My neighbors in Capernaum? My cousin Isaac? The guys I fish with?"

Jesus cost Peter temporary popularity, but Jesus promised Peter eternal pleasure at God's right hand (Psalm 16:11).

Let's take that idea back to the chart we just explored. This time, be honest about the wonderful things the people in your life can offer you and set those gains next to every spiritual gift that is yours in Christ. This time I'll help you with a few Bible passages before asking you to figure out which blessings are greater.

God's Gifts	> or < ?	Their Gifts
"Praise be to the God and Father of our Lord Jesus Christ, who has blessed us in the heavenly realms with every spiritual blessing in Christ" (Ephesians 1:3).		My parents give me . . .
"In love he predestined us for adoption to son-ship through Jesus Christ, in accordance with his pleasure and will—to the praise of his glorious grace, which he has freely given us in the One he loves" (Ephesians 1:4–6)		My best friend gives me . . .
"In him we have redemp-tion through his blood, the forgiveness of sins, in accordance with the riches of God's grace that he lavished on us" (Ephe-sians 1:7–8).		My significant other gives me . . .
"And you also were in-cluded in Christ when you heard the message of truth, the gospel of your salvation" (Ephesians 1:13).		My classmates/coworkers give me . . .
"When you believed, you were marked in him with a seal, the promised Holy Spirit, who is a deposit guaranteeing our inheri-tance until the redemption of those who are God's possession—to the praise of his glory" (Ephesians 1:13–14).		My teachers/professors give me . . .

God's Gifts	> or < ?	Their Gifts
"Praise be to the God and Father of our Lord Jesus Christ, who has blessed us in the heavenly realms with every spiritual blessing in Christ" (Ephesians 1:3).		My _____ gives me . . .

No disrespect to your people, but what is a lifetime of their blessing compared to being God's chosen, predestined, loved, redeemed, forgiven, included, marked, sealed, Spirit-filled people? His > Theirs!

Then > Now

The other day, I bought a 150-foot rope off of Amazon, wrapped a snippet of black tape around the first two inches of one end, and got ready to preach on the worthiness of God.

The gist of my message was this—Then > Now. While this life with all of its people, places, and things is filled with thrilling ups and difficult downs, it is minuscule compared to the eternal life that awaits the people of God. The happiness of hearing your name praised at work is euphoric, but it is short lived. The sting of being ignored because you won't flaunt your body at the beach is brutal, but it is a blink on the timeline of eternity.

Keeping this duration in mind is what gives your soul depth. The people of this world are living for that brief inch of black tape, grasping for as much pleasure, power, and approval as possible. But the people of the Word believe that there is more to life, much more, and that the life after this one endures forever. Faith reaches down to the depths of eternity, calculating the path to maximum happiness, acceptance, and approval.

This is how Jesus himself encouraged first-century churches who were facing the pain of persecution. While he didn't use a 150-foot rope, our King did say things like:

Be faithful, even to the point of death, and I will give you life as your victor's crown.

Revelation 2:10

To the one who is victorious and does my will to the end, I will give authority over the nations.

Revelation 2:26

The one who is victorious will, like them, be dressed in white. I will never blot out the name of that person from the book of life, but will acknowledge that name before my Father and his angels.

Revelation 3:5

The one who is victorious I will make a pillar in the temple of my God. Never again will they leave it. I will write on them the name of my God and the name of the city of my God.

Revelation 3:12

To the one who is victorious, I will give the right to sit with me on my throne, just as I was victorious and sat down with my Father on his throne.

Revelation 3:21

Those who endure, unashamed of Jesus and his words, will sit with the King of kings, dressed in white, wearing the crown of life, loved by God, and victoriously bearing his name. Jesus will invite us not to snap a quick selfie next to the throne but to spend forever in his presence, using every second of eternity to grasp the height and width and depth of his love.

You will never find a soul in heaven who says, "I wish I would have sold out Jesus." No! Instead, every Christian gazing at the face of Christ, even those who were rejected and crucified for his name, joins the chorus and shouts, "Worthy is the Lamb, who was slain, to receive power and wealth and wisdom and strength and honor and glory and praise!" (Revelation 5:12).

The founding pastor of the church I now serve used to encourage God's people with a similar equation: STP = LTP. Short-term pleasure equals long-term pain. Sometimes the stuff that feels really good in the moment, such as seeing a friend nod her head in agreement with your beliefs, feels so good. But when the friend is gone and there is just Jesus, how would it feel?

Then the pastor would add that STP = LTP. Short-term pain equals long-term pleasure. Losing a friend, a promotion, or the respect of your own family is painful, yet the pain is not in vain. Suffering for Jesus never is.

The Gain of Pain

These three truths—He > Them, His > Theirs, Then > Now—can actually take the pain of the world's rejection and turn it into your spiritual gain.

When your belief that God creates and defines life within the womb is labeled as anti-woman, anti-justice, and pro-patriarchy, let the scorn of the world drive you deeper into the nature and promises of God. "Why am I suffering for these words? Oh, yes, because the One who wrote them is worthy!"

Or when your religious yet racist uncle refuses to be corrected, calling you naive, sensitive, and liberal, let his unfair words push you into the arms of Jesus, a Middle Eastern Savior who had no intentions of idolizing northern European culture.

When Jesus' simple statement—"[God's] word is truth" (John 17:17)—is met with the torches and pitchforks of those who claim that truth is within, theirs to define, and not some

Book's or some God's, remember that you have lost their respect only because you have his. And he is worthy.

Yes, there is pain. But this type of pain is small compared to what we have gained through Jesus.

No, this doesn't give you the right to be a jerk for Jesus. You don't get to drop "truth bombs" on people living for the things of this world. May your heart be as broken as Jesus', who mourned when his enemies rejected him (Matthew 23:37), and your soul be as desperate as Paul, who was willing to trade his eternity for the salvation of those who thought he was crazy (Romans 9:2–3).

Continue to pray with passion, live like Jesus, and never give up loving those who don't love the Lord. But when their scorn beats down like the desert sun and you feel your joy starting to wither, tell your soul to reach down to the deep truths of the Word.

God is worthy. This is worth it.

Three Stories of Deep-Soil Souls

Thankfully, the history of the Christian church is filled with people who have believed that God is absolutely worth the pain. Consider the stories of the apostles, Polycarp of Smyrna, and Becket Cook.

In the first century, soon after Jesus returned to heaven, the apostles were arrested for proclaiming the name of their Messiah. After the apostles refused to keep quiet about the risen Christ, the local authorities decided to flog them (Acts 5:40).

Just in case you haven't seen a flogging in a while, this form of torture was grisly enough to earn Mel Gibson's movie about Jesus an R rating, an odd designation for a movie about a guy who never cursed, killed, or hooked up. If you can keep your eyes open through the scene, you'll see that flogging was an extreme form of whipping where sharp pieces of metal or bone were attached to the end of long leather straps. This weapon would dig into human flesh and rip back layers of tissue, showing no mercy to nerves, bones, and blood vessels. This is what happened to the apostles when they proclaimed the name of Jesus.

So did the fresh seed of the Christian church wither? To the contrary, Dr. Luke writes, "The apostles left the Sanhedrin, rejoicing because they had been counted worthy of suffering disgrace for the Name" (Acts 5:41).

Rejoicing! Picture James and John, dripping with blood, high-fiving despite the grimacing pain. Imagine Thaddeus trying to do a happy dance despite the bruises spreading around his ribs. These men were tortured and disgraced, but they knew exactly why—"the Name."

The name of Jesus was worth it. They had found "new life" and the "forgiveness of sins," which meant that Jesus > the world (Acts 5:20; 10:43).

A century later, an 86-year-old man said the same thing. Polycarp of Smyrna, according to the second-century historian Irenaeus, met the apostle John and fell in love with the name of Jesus soon after. Originally from Greece, Polycarp became a bishop in the early church and helped spread the name of Jesus to new places and new people.

But in those days, many people hated the exclusive claims of Jesus of Nazareth. People who refused to call Caesar "Lord" and vow their allegiance to the empire and its gods were threats to divine blessings and national security. Thus, old Polycarp's time of testing arrived.

His enemies tracked down the bishop, by this time in his mid-80s, and forced him into a stadium, where they threatened to unleash wild beasts upon his body unless he cursed the name of Jesus. But Polycarp would not, could not, curse Jesus, his greatest blessing.

When the authorities changed their threat and promised to burn him alive at the stake, this follower of Jesus declared, "You threaten a fire that burns for a time and is quickly extinguished." In other words, Then > Now.

When the rabid mob had gathered the logs, Polycarp prayed, "O Father of your beloved Son, Jesus Christ, I bless you. . . . I bless and glorify you through the eternal high priest, Jesus Christ, your beloved Son, through whom be glory to you and the Holy Spirit, both now and in the ages to come. Amen."[1]

The flame was lit, but his roots reached down and took hold of the worth of the One who saved him from sin and promised him eternal life. The old man died, but, in the process, discovered the life that is truly life.*

Two millennia after this martyr's death, another soul suffered for his faith in Jesus. Becket Cook was a successful set designer in Hollywood's fashion industry, a man who worked with stars, supermodels, and even partied with Paris Hilton and Prince himself.

But in 2009, while grabbing coffee with a friend in L.A., Becket noticed a group of people chatting over open Bibles. A conversation turned into an invitation, which ended up in Becket's conversion. His assumptions about religion were undone when he learned that Christianity offers salvation as a freely given gift, not, like the cutthroat culture of Hollywood, as a contract that must be earned or deserved.

Becket heard the goodness of the good news and became a proud follower of Jesus Christ.

But not everyone was thrilled by his new life. He had come to believe that Jesus was worth prioritizing, which meant that all his old passions, desires, and behaviors would bend the knee to his new, gracious King, submitting to Jesus' word in grateful obedience. This reorganization of his desires was anything but good news to friends who believed that They > God and that Now > Then.

Cook later wrote, "[Jesus] did cost me some friends, some really deep, lifelong relationships. A lot of my friends were

---

* Polycarp, by the way, is a name that literally means "much fruit."

semi-supportive, but some of my closest friends were not. . . . I was cut off from several people, some of the closest friends of my life."[2]

How do you deal with the pain of losing the respect of, even a relationship with, the people you love? Here's how Becket answered that question—"The gain is this relationship with God through Christ. Eternal life. It's this impenetrable joy because of not only knowing Christ but knowing the meaning of life—where I came from, what I'm doing, where I'm going. It gives me such peace."[3]

What was true for 21st-century followers, 2nd-century martyrs, and 1st-century apostles is true for you too, no matter how painful the sun of their persecution might feel.

He > Them. His > Theirs. Then > Now.

STUDY QUESTIONS

1. Do you know anyone who used to be excited about Jesus but lost their passion? What happened to wither their initial joy?

2. Based on your immediate family, your closest friends, and the current values of our culture, list the five teachings of the Bible that are most likely to spark a negative reaction. What will these teachings cost you as you go through life? Be honest. "In the same way, those of you who do not give up everything you have cannot be my disciples" (Luke 14:33).

3. Evaluate this statement: When it comes to Christianity, expectations are everything.

4. Those who are ignorant of the church's history easily forget what brothers and sisters have endured for the sake of Jesus. In order to strengthen your courage, do some online research of Christians who have suffered for Christ while declaring the worthiness of his name. Find examples, both ancient and modern, as a reminder that Jesus is worth whatever he costs you.

5. Besides He > Them, His > Theirs, and Then > Now, can you think of any other reasons to stick with the Word even when it is mocked by the world?

6. Challenge: In the next month, read the book of Acts. Keep a journal of (1) the names of all the Christians you meet, (2) what their connection to Jesus cost them, and (3) how they dealt with the threat of pain and persecution.

5

Worries

Other seed fell among thorns, which grew up and choked the plants, so that they did not bear grain. . . . The seed that fell among thorns stands for those who hear, but as they go on their way they are choked by life's worries, riches and pleasures, and they do not mature.

Mark 4; Luke 8, selected verses

Busy, Busy, Busy

We are busy people.

On second thought, that sentence doesn't do justice to the kind of people that most of us are. More accurately, we are busy, busy, busy people.

In early 2014, the BBC shared an article regarding sleep habits in modern culture. "A group of researchers discovered that we are sleeping between one and two hours less per night than people did sixty years ago, and two and a half hours less than a hundred years ago."[1]

Two and a half hours?! How in the world did our great-grandparents have so much extra time?*

But our lifestyle isn't just about shorter nights; it's also about cluttered days. From extracurriculars to AP classes to club sports to catching up on emails, most of our days are stretched tighter than an XS crop top on an oversized hippo.

This is true for church people too. You can believe God is worthy and still be very busy.

But, according to Jesus, your busy is a threat to your blessing.

Three Thoughts about Thorns

In the next part of Jesus' parable, we find seemingly good ground. Unlike the hardened path and the rocky soil, this spot has potential. This isn't a parking lot or a desert, devoid of plant life, but ground covered in green, evidence of its ability to grow and produce fruit.

But fruit isn't the only thing that grows from good ground. Thorns do too.

Based on my experience of trying to keep my yard from turning into a backyard jungle, there are three things I have learned about thorns that I want to pass on to you:

First, thorns just grow. Unless Kim is buying bulk orders of thistles and planting them while I'm sleeping, thorns just show up in our garden like the junk mail you didn't sign up for that ends up at your address nonetheless.

Second, thorns are painful to remove. Jesus' crown of thorns wasn't a cashmere cap. Thorns pick and poke and gouge and goad, especially if you need to grab them tightly enough to rip them up from the roots.

Finally, thorns threaten plant production. There is only so much sun, soil, and water for each square foot of ground, mean-

---

* The answer might be that they didn't play Madden or watch every episode of *The Office.*

ing that the garden is a zero-sum game. Let those thorns grow up, and your cucumbers will end up as skinny pickles, forced on a diet by their prickly competitors.

I wish those three truths weren't true, but this is what life has been like since Adam and Eve took the fruit and God explained the curse: "[The ground] will produce thorns and thistles for you" (Genesis 3:18). Thorns and thistles are the hard part of life after Eden.

Just like your spiritual life. Apply the three previous truths to the soil of your soul:

Busy just happens—in our world, busyness is our default setting, something that occurs without our intention. You don't need a New Year's resolution to rush more and sleep less. Seven miles over the limit is just the flow of traffic in our culture, and, without a countercultural intention, you will end up just as overbooked and underproductive as the average person.

Resisting busy is painful—giving your soul the space it needs to produce fruit will dig sharp thorns into tender skin, leaving part of you bleeding and crying, "But I can't stop doing *that*!" Saying no to the world and yes to the Word might sound inspirational, but it will feel like thick gloves, sharp thorns, and back sweat dripping down onto your underwear.

Not busy is necessary—Jesus said that cluttered soil "did not bear grain," meaning that cluttered souls "do not mature . . . making [them] unfruitful." Remember that these words were Jesus' loving warning not to church skippers but "for those who hear" the Word yet are too busy to be exponentially blessed.

The Holy Spirit longs to fill us with a supernatural peace and a profound joy that comes from our connection to Jesus, but that will never happen as long as the thorns of this life choke out the Word that we have heard. Good fruit requires a good chunk of time, the very thing busyness prevents.

What exactly are the thorns that keep us so busy? Jesus lists three—the worries of this life, the deceitfulness of wealth, and wanting other things.

In this chapter, we will address the first one on Jesus' list before tackling the others in the upcoming chapters.

Ready to work on your busy?

Worry Much?

To understand Jesus' warning about worries, you need only look to one of Jesus' dearest friends, Martha.

I get Martha. While the Bible doesn't list her personality type, she strikes me as an Enneagram 1 or 3, a woman who wants everything to be perfect and everyone to be impressed by her work. When Jesus and his friends showed up at her home, she didn't toss a few pizza rolls into the oven and tell the apostles to BYOB.* Instead, Martha wanted to give her Messiah her first and her best.

So she did. She worried, I imagine, about finding a chair fitting for the King of kings, about what dishes to set out for the Host of heaven's feast, about what food to offer the Bread of Life, and what drink to pour for the Giver of living water. Those worries, as admirable as they were, left Martha's brain cluttered. As she rushed here and there, she heard the words of Jesus from the other room, seeds plump with potential, but her soul was overgrown with everything else that had to be done.

Had to. That's what Martha thought (Luke 10:40). "I would have slowed down, but I *had to* get things done. What other option did I have?"

Jesus, in one of his most tender moments, spoke to his frazzled friend. "'Martha, Martha,' the Lord answered, 'you are worried and upset about many things, but few things are needed—or indeed only one'" (Luke 10:41–42).

---

* I can't theologically confirm this, but I am convinced that Jesus would have loved pizza rolls. Everyone I have ever met who is filled with the Spirit does.

You are *worried*. There's that same word that showed up two chapters earlier in Jesus' parable: "[Some people] are choked by life's worries . . . and they do not mature" (Luke 8:14).

In her helpful work on feminine anxiety, author Sissy Goff writes, "The most anxious girls I see are often the busiest."[2] Anxiety sometimes comes from a responsible, selfless mind that is racing everywhere to do everything and please everyone. The unintended consequence, however, is that we never quite mature enough to enjoy the fruits of peace, joy, and love.

But in his gentle correction of Martha, Jesus is giving us permission to change a few "have tos" into "used tos." We don't have to. We might choose to if there's time and space, but we don't have to, because few things are needed. In fact, only one thing is needed.

The seed.

Before we explore the potential of an uncluttered life, consider which worries might be choking out God's Word from the space it needs to grow in your heart. Grab a pen or a highlighter and mark the three statements that your Martha-ish heart is tempted to believe enough to keep you busy.

1. I'm worried that if I don't get all *A*s, I'll be considered average, get passed over for the scholarship, and end up with crippling college debt for the next ten years.

2. I'm worried that if I don't have enough volunteer hours, extracurriculars, and foreign language credits, my preferred college won't accept my application and I'll fall behind my peers.

3. I'm worried that if I don't reply to this text right away, keep up this Snapchat streak, and reply to these emails before bed, my friends will think I don't care about them.

4. I'm worried that if I don't show up early, stay late, say yes to everything the company wants, and return my

manager's emails within an hour (no matter what the hour), I'll lose my reputation at work.

5. I'm worried that if I don't attend church on Sunday and Bible study on Monday and the midweek service on Wednesday, the members of my church will think less of me.

6. I'm worried that if I don't go to the Christmas parties and find a fun Christmas sweater and write a funny Christmas letter and design a customized Christmas card while baking homemade Christmas cookies for the midweek Christmas service, I will make the baby Jesus cry.*

7. I'm worried that if I say no to going to the party, to joining them for coffee, and to attending the wedding, people will consider me selfish.

8. I'm worried that if I don't get my kid involved in club sports early, she will never make varsity and will miss the fun I had being involved with high school athletics.

9. I'm worried that if I take a break from social media, I'll disappoint my friends and family.

10. I'm worried that I can't slow down, or I would fail God.

Personally, I can relate to most of that list. Can you?

This is life in a world where busyness replaces fruitfulness and thinning out our schedule feels like wearing a crown of thorns.

Comma But

In studying Jesus' story, I ended up binging about 20 sermons on the parable of the sower, searching for fresh insights from the gospel texts. My favorite came from a preacher in California who pointed out the phrase "comma but."

Jesus said, "The seed that fell among thorns stands for those who hear, but . . ." (Luke 8:14).

---

* After all, what would the birth of Christ be without an ugly sweater and a sugary cookie?

Such potential! Those who hear the Word can believe the Word, enjoy the Word, and apply the Word. That seed, once heard, can set down deep roots and produce delicious fruit. They hear, but . . .

Comma but.

In our lives, this might sound like . . .

"Sunday's message honestly moved me, but then we had to rush out the door to make it to practice on time."

"I know God is urging me to honor my aging parents with some extra time, but I have stuff going on four nights a week."

"I would love to slow down for my morning devotion, but there is just so much to do."

Comma but.

I wish I could offer you a shortcut to maturity, but the law of the garden applies to your life too—fruit requires space. Scripture can't be squeezed into a cluttered life. To mature and produce fruit, we will have to do the painful work of pulling out the thorns of "comma but."

How Did We Get So Busy?

How did we end up sleep-deprived, overbooked, and so darn busy? For most of us, it wasn't something as big and obvious as a second full-time job or a double major but rather the cluttering nature of "just a little."

Isn't that true? A little commitment to coaching, another little meeting to attend, another Saturday away from home, and, little by little, we end up with a life we never intended and a garden that will never be able to grow into what God intends. Jesus' "comma but" comes from "just a little."

In order not to get lost in generalities, let's make this personal. In the space on the next page, do the math of your average week, counting up how many hours you spend sleeping, working, studying, scrolling, cooking, etc. If you're going to do the urgent work of pulling up some thorns, we need to figure out what those thorns actually are.

	Sunday	Monday	Tuesday	Wednesday	Thursday	Friday	Saturday	Total
Sleep								
School								
Work								
TV								
Social Media								
Gaming								
Friends								
Family								
Fitness								
Chores								
Church								
Other:								

As you look back at the numbers, ask yourself, "How did I end up like this? What was I so worried about that I ended up so overcommitted?"

Ready for the harder question? It comes from another Scripture about thorns: "The way of the sluggard is blocked with thorns" (Proverbs 15:19).

"Sluggard" seems a bit harsh to describe our lives,* but consider the connection between a busy life and a thorn-filled garden. Both are under the oversight of someone who doesn't want to do painful work.

And, trust me, getting yourself un-busy will be painful. What is much, much easier is to throw some extra seeds in that cluttered garden and hope this batch brings back more fruit than the last one. Read another chapter, attend another service, find another podcast about Jesus.

* I dare you to call someone a sluggard today. "How dare you, you sluggard!"

I'm all for hearing the Word, but . . . * your garden might not need more of anything right now, but less.

So let's pray for strength and start to rip up some thorns.

The Answer to Worry

Last spring, Kim and I laced up our old, grass-stained tennis shoes and planted our annual garden. She handed me a hoe and told me to follow the directions on the seed packets that she had purchased from the local hardware store.

Each packet explained how deep to trench the soil and how many days the seed would take to germinate, information that I would expect. What I didn't expect, however, was that each seed maker also listed the "seed spacing" or, as some packets put it, the "thin to" distance. Apparently, more seeds do not equal more fruit, since seeds, by their nature, require space and soil to mature and grow.

Sound familiar?

Jesus didn't put a nifty chart on the packet we call the Bible, but he did teach us that seeds need to breathe, requiring us to thin out our lives and give the Spirit some space to produce fruit. In the kingdom of God, less now often leads to more then.

This is why I will be eternally grateful to my hometown pastor.

When I was approaching my seminary graduation, my hometown pastor gave me some shocking advice that would eventually change my life. He told me, "Mike, when you get to your first church, ask the leaders there how many hours you should work."

"Um," I objected, "that sounds like terrible advice. They'll think I'm lazy! There is no way I am going to ask them for the minimum threshold of hours I need to work so they don't get mad at me. Ever heard of making a good first impression?"

"No," his wisdom objected to my objection, "you need to establish some mutual expectations. Otherwise, you'll work 70

* Notice that comma and conjunction?

hours a week and someone will get mad that you didn't show up for 'their thing.'"

So within the first few months at the church that welcomed this clueless shepherd, I told the leadership team, with fear and trembling, "I'm afraid to bring this up, but my mentor said I had to. I really want to be a blessing to this church. I don't want to burn out. I don't want to fake having a strong marriage or end up with kids who hate the church because their church-serving father was never home. I want to love people here out of the overflow of my own healthy relationship with Jesus. So if you all wanted to be close to Jesus, loving spouses, and good parents, how many hours could you work?"

To my pastor's credit (and to the credit of the Christians in the room), no one misunderstood my honest question. Instead, person by person, they shared how many hours would work in their own lives—40, 50, 45, 55, 40, 45, etc. In the end, we decided that, while circumstances and seasons might require more hours on any given week, my goal would be to work 50 faithful hours every seven days for our congregation.

That number, it turns out, would produce immense amounts of fruit.

While other pastors I knew burned out, I felt fresh. While surveys revealed that many pastors had no personal devotional lives, no emotional intimacy with their wives, and too few dinners at their own kitchen table, God had given me the space to enjoy his Word every day, to date my wife every week, and to disciple my children over home-cooked meals and unrushed devotions.

Even now, I get choked up thinking of the gift my pastor gave me—an unchoked life.

Maintaining that pace for the past 14 years hasn't always been easy, since the people pleaser in me defaults to yes when face-to-face with a passionate person and their passionate ideas. But structuring my life with intentional space has proven to be fruitful—I still love my work, have an imperfect/amazing marriage, am blessed with a network of close friends, and spend quantity time with my soon-to-be-teenage daughters.

Pastor, thank you for your crazy advice. It has produced a hundred times more than I imagined.

So perhaps I could pass the baton of wisdom that my mentor passed on to me. You might not be a pastor facing the church council, but is there some way that you could create space to be your best at what matters most?

Look back at your time audit. Is there anything, honestly, that wouldn't kill you to stop doing? I know it would be painful, like pulling out a clump of thorns, but could you swallow hard, step back, and give the seed some space to breathe?

Our world won't make that easy, but the Word wants so much more for you. God wants to spend time with you, not just quality but quantity time, time when he has your full attention and your phone in airplane mode. Jesus wants to look you in the eyes and remind you just how much you've been forgiven, just how deeply you are loved, and just how unbelievable God's plans for you are.

No quick glances at the clock to see if you're late. No phone buzzing in your pocket to rush to the next "have to." No hearing Jesus until "comma but." Just space. Just time. So the Spirit can speak and you can believe and be blessed.

There Is Nothing Else

Pastor John Ortberg once recounted a conversation he had with Dallas Willard, a man some have called a spiritual giant of his generation. Ortberg's church was bursting at the seams and his personal life was crammed with soccer games and too many school events, so he reached out to Willard for help. "What should I do to become spiritually healthy?" Ortberg asked.

After a thoughtful pause, Willard responded, "You must ruthlessly eliminate hurry from your life."

Like a good student, Ortberg scribbled down that first piece of advice. Then, hoping for something more profound, he asked, "What else is there?"

Willard paused again. "There is nothing else."[3]

I wonder if Willard learned that from Jesus. Spiritual maturity is possible for every hearer of the Word, just like every seed contains the potential for roots, stems, blossoms, and fruit. But both require a ruthless commitment to clear out the clutter.

As you consider your own schedule, let me speak a word to busy parents and to the compassionate souls among us.

Dear Parents,

I have a new appreciation for the tension that modern parents feel. When my daughters were little, life was crazy, but the crazy felt containable. Yes, we had to figure out potty training.* Yes, we had to survive upside-down sleep schedules, handle public tantrums, and convince our girls that biting other children wasn't okay with Jesus.

But Kim and I never really argued about parenting until middle school. That's when the sports began.

In my day,† sports were a pastime, not a part-time job. I played both varsity and college soccer despite only a little club ball during my teenage summers. Grade school soccer? I never played it. Special camps? Maybe one in my whole life. I wasn't some fútbol prodigy; that was just how things were in the '90s.

But this is not the '90s. Recently, my 12-year-old daughter had to choose between the club volleyball team that had 8 weekend tournaments, the other team that had 10 weekend tournaments, and the other, other team that had 12 weekend

---

* We bribed our firstborn with M&M's, her younger sister with summer sausage. I never thought a man with a master's degree would say, "If you go poopie in the potty, Daddy will give you some sausage."

† After typing those three words, I am officially accepting that I am not young anymore.

tournaments. Eight to twelve weekends! Did I mention she is 12?! Did I mention she isn't an only child?! Did I mention that Kim and I both have full-time jobs?!

Being the sassy padre that I am, I scoffed at the commitment level of the club sports culture. I even recounted what sports were like "in my day."

But my wife explained the new normal and how our kid's ability to play sports at her future high school was likely dependent on our family's willingness to spend 8 to 12 weekends sitting on bleachers and buying Little Caesars on the car ride home.

Kim had a point. I love playing soccer to this day, so I see the long-term value of team sports and want my children to enjoy some of those same blessings. But the thought of the cost kills me.

Moms and dads out there, I feel for you. A cluttered schedule isn't just for elite athletes and grad school students but for average families that just want their kids to make friends, stay healthy, and share the experiences we had growing up.

But when I think of what Jesus taught and what his Father valued, it forces me to take a painful, countercultural step and say, *Please, pull up those thorns. For the sake of your fruit— your love and kindness and joy—and for the sake of their fruit—their peace and patience and gentleness—do the painful work of saying no to anything that would stunt your family's spiritual maturity.*

Your babies don't know this yet, but when they are old, they won't care much about making it to the championship bracket. They will care about the salsa you taught them to make on another unrushed evening, the safety they felt when you were home for the night, the peace of not juggling 72 to-dos in their brains.

They don't want a medal. They want a mom.

They don't want first place. They want a father.

They don't need a weekend in a gym. They need forever with Jesus.

So be a rebel. Be the family whose wrinkles come from laughter and not from stress. Invest your time in being together instead of rushing apart.

You can do this. God wants this. That's why he scattered this seed in your direction.

Dear Compassionate People,

I admire you.

I mean that. When I think of all the things I am good at (running, kicking, reading, talking) and all the things I am not good at (compassion, empathy, selflessness), I deeply admire people like you. The Bible has much more flattering things to say about you than it does about me.

My mother and my youngest daughter are like you. They would do anything for anyone, no matter what the hour or the cost. When I see their big hearts for people, I think of Jesus' unfailing love and the Father's bottomless love for us.

But equal to my admiration is my concern for you. Because bighearted people, in my experience, often lack boundaries, leaving them with full schedules and not-so-fruitful lives. It's hard to really rejoice when so many people are counting on you, just as it's hard to be at peace when there are so many more people who still need a helping hand.

If that's you, let me take a bit of that burden from you by reminding you of Jesus.

Jesus was love on two legs. If you have any doubt about his compassion, watch as he lifts little children up in his arms, interrupts his itinerary to minister to desperate outcasts, and isn't ashamed to defend an adulteress woman in front of the local pastors. James said of his big brother Jesus, "The Lord is full of compassion and mercy" (James 5:11).

But Jesus, despite his compassionate agenda, still had space.

Just imagine the day the lines stretched along the shores of the

98

Sea of Galilee as every village within walking distance brought their sick, their lame, and their demon-possessed to Jesus. With grace and truth, Jesus broke fevers, tossed out crutches, and told the demons to go back to hell. But as the sun set and the line lengthened, Jesus did the most unexpected thing.

He left.

The moment arrived when Jesus turned to his friends and said, "Let us go over to the other side [of the sea]" (Mark 4:35). When the Savior decided it was time to bounce, was every need met just yet? Mark answers, "Leaving the crowd behind, they took him along, just as he was, in the boat" (Mark 4:36).

Jesus left the crowd behind. Some desperate soul was still in line, having waited all day for healing, finally next up for the Great Physician's miraculous touch.

But Jesus left. And yet the Lord remained sinless.

That little detail, which happens to appear in the same chapter as the parable of the sower, might be just what you need to say no without guilt backing up a dump truck to your heart. God never intended for you to help everyone any more than Jesus believed he had to work the third shift to appease the crowds.

Be like Jesus. Say no and get into the boat that takes you away from the dings and the beeps and the needs. Take a nap after hours of faithful service, like Jesus did. Escape to a quiet place to pray, like Jesus did. Prioritize time with your Father, allowing him to meet the deepest needs of your soul.

Doing so doesn't make you a selfish person. It makes you just like Jesus.

A Final Thought about Thorns

In scanning the Bible for passages about thorns, I discovered a great gospel connection, one that you might need about now if your busy life is burdening your conscience. Here goes—

Jesus took your thorns.

Yes, thorns are connected to clutter, laziness, and immaturity. The writer to the Hebrews warns, "Land that produces thorns and thistles is worthless and is in danger of being cursed. In the end it will be burned" (Hebrews 6:8). These words snap us out of our busy, busy, busy stupor and remind us of God's goal for the soil of our hearts.

But before we despair, we remember the last words the gospels say about thorns—"When Jesus came out wearing the crown of thorns and the purple robe, Pilate said to them, 'Here is the man!'" (John 19:5). Where are the thorns that clutter my life, robbing me of growth? Where are your thorns, the ones that threaten you with God's curse?

They are on the sacred head of Jesus.

Nine hundred years ago, Bernard of Clairvaux wrote in his classic hymn, "O sacred head now wounded/With grief and shame weighed down/Now scornfully surrounded/With thorns your only crown/O sacred head, no glory/Now from your face does shine/Yet, though despised and gory/I joy to call you mine."[4]

Jesus was crowned with thorns so that the fruit of joy would be all yours. His thorny head allows you to lift up your head and rejoice that you are precious to the Gardener we call our Father.

May this grace inspire you to take Jesus' story to heart and consider how you might pull out your thorns, simplify your life, and find space you need to mature in your faith.

STUDY QUESTIONS

1. What worries keep you busy with nonessential things? Jot down five current examples, and then list them in order of the ones you worry about most.

2. What did you learn from the time audit in this chapter? If you have the courage, share the results with a mature Christian friend and ask for their candid reaction, opening your heart to any "have tos" that you could turn into "used tos."

3. Agree/Disagree—Culture shapes Christians more than we like to admit, especially when it comes to how we spend our time.

4. Study the parable of the great banquet from Luke 14:15–24, making at least three connections between Jesus' story and this chapter.

5. Evaluate: People who read too many Bible passages, listen to too many Christian podcasts, and watch too many Bible-based videos are robbing themselves of the space the Word needs to grow and mature in their minds.

6. Read Jesus' classic sermon on worry in Matthew 6:25–34. What worries does Jesus mention in these verses? How does seeking the Father's love allow us to let go of our worries and breathe in the peace that goes beyond understanding?

6

Wealth

Other seed fell among thorns, which grew up and choked the plants, so that they did not bear grain. . . . Still others, like seed sown among thorns, hear the word; but the worries of this life, the deceitfulness of wealth and the desires for other things come in and choke the word, making it unfruitful.

Mark 4, selected verses

Tupperware Tales

In theory, I like Tupperware. Tupperware enables my family to save, store, and reheat leftovers at an extremely affordable price. I'm trying to imagine life without Tupperware, and it feels wasteful and complicated.*

But my six hundred-piece Tupperware life is complicated too.

Okay, I don't have six hundred pieces of Tupperware, but every time I open that particular cabinet in my kitchen, I

---

* What do you do with extra stir fry? Throw it out? Put it in an unmicrowavable Ziplock? Force yourself to finish it and tell God you're sorry for being a glutton?

wonder, "How did this happen?" How did I end up with this postapocalyptic scene of scattered lids and squares cluttered next to more squares and more lids? Who decided that stacking up the Leaning Tower of Tupperware was a wise idea? And which member of our family made the executive decision to buy approximately six times more Tupperware than we use in any given week? Were we hoping to avoid the embarrassment of running out of room if Jesus multiplied our stir fry and we didn't have the plastic containers to preserve his miracle?

How did we end up like this?

According to Jesus, we don't end up cluttered by intention but rather by lack of attention. Closets and kitchens are a lot like gardens, where thorns show up uninvited.

Jesus said the same thing about wealth. What should be a blessing can leave you stressing as money stops God's Word from producing the kind of joy and peace that the Father intended.

> The seed falling among the thorns refers to someone who hears the word, but the worries of this life and the deceitfulness of wealth choke the word, making it unfruitful.
>
> Matthew 13:22

Money, Money, Money

The Messiah wasn't anti-money. When Zacchaeus, a one percenter from Jericho, gave away half of his wealth to the poor, Jesus didn't judge him for holding on to the other half. Throughout his life, Jesus was blessed by rich men, funded by wealthy women, and reliant on the hospitality of homeowners who had room for him to crash on their couches (Matthew 9:10; Luke 8:3; Mark 2:1; Matthew 8:20).

In other words, Jesus' problem wasn't with dollars or denarii but with deception. He feared that many of us would hear the

Word, but before that seed could reach its potential, money would deceive us into, once again, being too busy to be blessed.

What is it, exactly, about money that keeps us constantly busy chasing more of it? Why does green not always look good on us but always looks good to us?

Perhaps it's because money promises to give us a new and better life. My Grandma Novotny used to say, "It's just money. The pigs won't even eat it!" No disrespect to my dear grandmother, but she wasn't entirely correct. More money gives us more of the blessings we truly enjoy in this life. Consider seven examples.

Seven Promises That Money Makes

1. More money = More experiences

We adore experiences. Those three words are one of my family's stated values, which is why we drive rusty used cars so that we can explore this big, beautiful world. In the past decade, my girls have met Elsa at Disney, stood on the edge of the Grand Canyon, and held a live Honduran sloth in their arms.

These experiences were incredible. And they cost a good chunk of money.

Unless Expedia gives you a 100% off code, seeing the wonderful world that God made will not be free. If you only had more money, you could dip your toes in the ocean, try a croissant in Paris, and see the very places where Jesus lived, died, and was raised.

Money might not make the world go 'round, but money can get you around the world.

2. More money = More comfort

During a search for some workout equipment, my family ended up in a local strip mall shop that sold exercise stuff and, to my surprise/delight, massage chairs. I wasn't aware that the dumbbell store carried high-end mechanical masseuses, but I took advantage of the opportunity to sit down and test drive this five-figure piece of furniture.

Trying to describe the ecstasy of those few minutes would be like trying to describe parental love to a preschooler. I can assure you, however, that it got awkward when my entire family was waiting at the door and the employee wondered why the middle-aged man in Adidas pants was still sitting in the chair that he obviously didn't have the funds to purchase.*

Money can make you comfortable, can't it? From a pillow-top mattress to well-made shoes, driver's seats with booty warmers to cashmere sweaters, a shower with fancy pressure settings to new furniture that induces naps upon contact, extra cash can keep you extra comfortable.

3. More money = More respect

People respect people who have money. The woman who can afford a high-end salon cut and color gets extra attention and applause. So does the donor who gives a five-figure gift to a local nonprofit. And so does the couple who pulls up to the stoplight in a two-seat convertible that they just drove off the lot.

People notice money, and something in us loves to be noticed.

4. More money = More security

You would feel the difference if you slept on a park bench one week and slept in a secure home the next. Those without a dollar in their pocket are left vulnerable to the people and problems of this world, while those who have five-figure savings accounts have layers of security. A house in a safer neighborhood. An alarm system on every door and window. An emergency fund so you don't have to worry about increased insurance or dropped transmissions. An emergency fund for your emergency fund

---

* If any of you kind readers would like to donate $10,000 to the Mike Novotny Experiences Heaven in a Chair Fund, I would gladly receive your probably-not-tax-deductible gift.

so you can weather company cutbacks, a market crash, and unexpected medical bills.

Live paycheck to paycheck and you are always one step away from financial danger. But get your hands on more money and you can keep danger at a distance.

5. More money = More opportunity

Few can deny the extra doors that open when you have an impressive résumé. While high school dropouts can absolutely make a difference in this world, many doors are closed and locked unless you have a track record of education to prove your potential. But if you haven't heard the rumors just yet, college and grad school cost more than a fancy massage chair.

I bet your opportunities aren't free either. Your dream to become a nurse or a writer or an architect is dependent on degrees, which depend on dollars. Your passion to open your own restaurant or start your nonprofit or market your artwork will never become a reality without real money. That master's in education or PhD in psychology could be God's way of maximizing your spiritual gifts, but unlike eternal life, those blessings are by works and not by grace.

But if you could make enough and save enough, doors would open. Money would give you opportunity.

6. More money = More rest

I don't know many people who hate having time off. Even the sternest guy at work smiles when it's his last day before vacation.

When your mailbox is filled with overdue utility bills and reminders of upcoming payments, you can't take time off or retire early. Your creditors demand that you grind it out, cut back on expenses, and pay back what you owe them. But with enough money, you could stop running and start resting, letting your savings and retirement accounts fund your afternoon on the golf course and your lazy week watching the grandkids.*

If you could just make x, you could drop your second job. If you could just reach y, you could retire by next summer. If you could just get more money, you would end up with more rest.

7. More money = More impact

One of the wonderful things about America's youngest generations is their sincere desire to make a difference. While becoming rich and famous still tempts too many teenagers, more and more seem to care deeply about ending sex trafficking, improving inner-city inequalities, and addressing the anxiety epidemic in our digital age.

And money can make that all happen. With enough funding, you could expand the frontline staff of a worthy nonprofit, support needed research for that rare autoimmune disorder, and offer free-of-charge counseling hours for those struggling with mental health. More money doesn't just promise fast cars and nice homes but sex slaves set free and orphans who have a chance to succeed.

No wonder we want more money.

Seven Facts Money Didn't Mention

If you were reading carefully, you might have noticed that none of money's promises were anti-Jesus. Our Father loves to bless us with experiences, comfort, respect, security, opportunity, rest, and impact as he gives us glimpses of heaven and helps us leverage our spiritual gifts.

This is why, perhaps, Jesus didn't talk in this parable about the "evil of wealth" or the "possession of wealth" but rather the "deceitfulness of wealth." Money's danger is in the fine print, and few Christians take time to read it. We are too busy

---

* Scratch that. No grandparent feels lazy after five days of chasing after a five-year-old.

to look for the terms and conditions, so we scroll down and sign, trusting that money has our best interests at heart.

But Jesus has spent his eternal existence watching thorns choke out his Word. That's why he warns us that money might not take our faith, but it just might stop our faith from reaching maturity. Like one of my favorite high school hits said, "Mo Money Mo Problems."*

Your desire for a better degree, a better job, and a better salary might come from a good place, but your eyes need to be wide open for what money might do to your spiritual maturity. In his commentary on Jesus' parable, Arthur Just Jr. writes, "Obsession with possessions can lead to [the Word's] slow death by suffocation."[1]

How so? Here are some not-so-wonderful things that money might have forgotten to mention to you.

1. You'll need time to get me.

This one should be obvious unless you bought that pyramid-scheme pitch that gaining wealth would be easy. If you want more money, you will need to work more hours. Part-time employees don't make full-time salaries, so plan on 40 hours being a slow week at work.

The reality is that big money requires a big commitment, and in our competitive culture, there will always be someone to hire who will sacrifice nights, weekends, and personal time to get the job done.

Money might leave you with less time than you thought.

2. You'll gain stress to deserve me.

When I was a teenager making $7.50 an hour, I would cut grass, pull weeds, spread mulch, and then go home. Once I

---

* I'm speaking of the 1997 hit by the Notorious B.I.G., Mase, and Puff Daddy, not the Damon Wayans comedic thriller *Mo' Money*. I have yet to see Mr. Wayans' movie because I am busy reorganizing my Tupperware.

punched out, my brain was free to think about God, girls, and video games.* I can't recall a single night when I stared at my Salisbury steak TV dinner and fretted about how much mulch there was left to spend.

But then I started to make double-digit-per-hour money, and I learned that my post-work brain was different. Now there were serious problems to solve, critics whose words echoed in my head, and decisions that would disappoint people whom I pastored. It became increasingly difficult to leave work at work.

Your high-paying dreams will do the same. One of the reasons some jobs pay big money is because you are taking on a big burden. Hiring and firing, budgets and board meetings, decisions and directions all end up on your desk. When the buck stops with you, you can make more bucks.

But how much do you bring home? How much joy is lost at church when your mind is elsewhere? How much love do you show when you can't listen to her because you're still thinking about them?

Did they mention that when they offered you the raise?

3. You'll spend weekends to spend me.

It's not just making money that can clutter your life; it's also spending it.

As a two-income family, we had the money to buy a new couch this year. After living with hand-me-down leftovers from generous churchgoers, Kim and I decided it was time to up our basement game and buy a couch that all four of our family members could snuggle up on.

Little did I know how much work it would be to buy one! First, we jumped onto Ikea's website and spent an hour picking our top three choices. Then, we stopped at Ikea to let our backs and backsides test the comfort level of our top picks. Dissatisfied,

---

* Which mostly happened in an alternate order.

we explored five other local furniture stores, spending half a Saturday and a quarter tank of gas to come up with a new leader board. Finally, we pulled the trigger and bought the couch.

Which arrived three months later.*

So do some imaginary math with me. Not only did Kim and I have to work x hours to afford the couch, we also had to spend y hours to actually get the couch.

This is the way it works with wealth. When you have money, you have options. You can choose from any car on the lot, any rack of the store, any vacation spot on the globe. Be blessed with more money, and you'll be cursed with the thorns of upgrading, renovating, and more.

Apparently, being busy Monday through Friday can make you busy Saturday and Sunday too.

4. You'll exhaust effort to maintain me.

Stuff is like a spouse. It's work to find a good one, but more work to keep it good.

When you buy a brand-new car, you probably wash it more often than I wash my 2006 Town & Country.† And when you decide on the house with the gorgeous yard, you probably work hard to keep the yard looking gorgeous. Above-average stuff requires above-average effort, which is rarely mentioned by the marketing types.

The Holy Spirit might love to produce an act of kindness in you this weekend, but how can you help your neighbor with his yard when you are so busy with your own?

5. You'll be busy managing me.

If you've ever managed or led an organization, you know that administrative work is a black hole that sucks in more time than you would prefer. The bigger something gets, the

---

* Thanks, Coronavirus.
† Which is zero times in the past nine years.

more structure it requires, and structures need management and maintenance.

If God gave you $1,000,000, the same thing would become true for you. You would need time to figure out a budget, organize your tax documents, and track your increasing pile of receipts. I don't imagine that homeless people spend much time tracking down 1098-MISC forms and trying to remember passwords for their online investments.

But you might. More money means more management.

6. You'll get moody protecting me.

Recently, my daughters and I ducked into a newer business on our downtown strip that sold expensive sneakers. Honestly, there were some pretty dope shoes in there.* One of the owners even told us about the $6,000 pair of limited-edition shoes that they kept in a glass case.

Imagine if you bought them, laced them up, and turned heads as you strutted the streets of downtown. And imagine how you'd feel the first time someone accidentally stepped on your toes and scuffed up the shoes that cost more than my last car!

Money's ability to prevent your maturity is often connected to the way you feel about nice stuff. It's hard to be patient, gentle, and kind when a friend spills merlot on your new couch, your baby niece stretches out your new sweater with her chubby hands, or the lady at Walmart dings her door into your new car.

In the end, Jesus loves it when you love. But it's hard to love people who mess with your nice stuff.

7. You'll worry about losing me.

My first car was a 1994 Geo Tracker loaded with a ten-disc CD changer and two subwoofers so big they took the place of

---

* Question: Can a 40-year-old use the word *dope*? If not, please insert an appropriate alternative.

the Geo's back seat.* But in addition to the expensive sound system, I also had an expensive alarm.

I was worried about my money.

Money and worry seem to hang out a lot together, don't they? The higher the value, the greater the loss, so you worry about what might happen in a world where stealing is so common God had to put it on his top-ten list. While a fruit of the Spirit is peace, it's hard to feel peace when people might take your stuff.†

Put those seven points together and you understand the complicated relationship between money and maturity. Earning more, spending more, and having more often leaves us with less time, energy, and love to produce up to our potential.

Maybe this is why Agur wrote, "Give me neither poverty nor riches, but give me only my daily bread. Otherwise, I may have too much and disown you and say, 'Who is the LORD?'" (Proverbs 30:8–9). And perhaps Jesus had these same words in mind when he taught us to pray for "daily bread" just before his essential teaching on money and worry (Matthew 6:11, 19–34).

As I pondered Jesus' words, I reached out to a fellow Christian who had been very successful in the business world. I wanted to know what his experience had been like in a high-paying, high-performance career. By God's grace, he had remained a Christian who loved Jesus and made time to attend, serve, and bless his local church. He was a hearer of the Word.

But he also confessed the cost of his success. He wrote, "As I progressed in my career, the job consumed more of my brain time. Hours did go up a bit to the point where a typical work-week was 55–60 hours. . . . My time in the Word was usually

---

* You younger readers don't even know how cool I was to have a CD changer that size.

† Not-So-Fun Fact: The Tracker used to belong to my older brother, and his entire sound system was stolen while we watched the original *Jurassic Park* at the local theater.

early morning before work. Honestly, I probably didn't meditate as much as just read the verses."

I give this man credit for prioritizing some daily time with Jesus. But I also wonder what might have been if he had made half the salary and had twice as much time to meditate on the cross of his Savior.

A friend of mine agreed. Despite being years younger than me, his career has been filled with six-figure jobs. I have always known him as a man of deep faith with a sense of priorities, so I was curious if his experience paralleled others that I had heard about.

He admitted, "Truthfully, this has been one of the bigger struggles I've had in my adult life. I feel guilty even saying that. . . . God has ridiculously blessed me in my career: the things I've learned, the responsibilities I've had, the people I've met, the people I've led, the promotions, the places I traveled (all over North America). I've closed multimillion-dollar deals. I've also dealt with the fear and uncertainty wondering whether I'd have a job after losing upwards of a $50,000,000 deal. I thought that the promotions and the raises would be more satisfying. The result is that I found myself more stressed and less able to unplug. . . . My actual working hours weren't unmanageable (maybe 45–50, but that would ebb and flow pending things going on and travel). The tradeoff, more so, was the stress. I wouldn't necessarily be at work, but I'd be answering a call, an email, having to duck out of dinner. Those were regular occurrences. I was constantly tied to my phone."

I appreciate the honesty of these two men, because I have found myself in the same place. When life is too busy and my brain is packed with tumbling piles of responsibilities, I still go to church and read my Bible. However, I miss out on meditation, deep thinking, and prayerful reflection, vital habits that produce fruit in my life.

Have you felt that too?

Blessed is the one . . . whose delight is in the law of the LORD, and who meditates on his law day and night. That person is like a tree planted by streams of water, which yields its fruit in season and whose leaf does not wither—whatever they do prospers.

Psalm 1:1–3

Why, Though?

Before we explore some answers to wealth's deceptive nature, let's do the thorn-removing work of asking ourselves, "Why?" If we know that money can't buy happiness, why do we end up so neck-deep in busyness?

The answer is the three enemies in Jesus' parable—the deceiver, the deceived, and the deceivable.

The Deceiver

Money is all too tempting because the devil is all too good at his job.

When Adam and Eve got duped by the devil, Eve admitted, "The serpent deceived me, and I ate" (Genesis 3:13). The apostle Paul described the same enemy and his same ability when he wrote, "Eve was deceived by the serpent's cunning" (2 Corinthians 11:3).

(This might just be a grammatical coincidence, but I noticed that you need to put an *i* in the middle of Eve to spell the word *deceive*.)

In his sly way, the deceiver uses half-truths about money to choke out three-quarters of our potential. He draws our eyes to the bottom line, whispering about the wonders of all those zeros, but he fails to mention what "more" will cost us. Thus, instead of making wise decisions, choosing less money for the sake of more patience, kindness, and peace, we take a bite, just like Eve. Without stopping to listen for his voice, we assume the promotion, the raise, and the potential that the company sees in us must be from the Father above instead of from the deceiver below.

But Jesus warned, "Watch out! Be on your guard against all kinds of greed; life does not consist in an abundance of possessions" (Luke 12:15). Watch out for his deception! Don't believe the lie that life—real life, a better life, the blessed life—is just one more dollar away.

Former US Vice President Al Gore once lamented, "The accumulation of material goods is at an all-time high, but so is the number of people who feel an emptiness in their lives."[2]

Emptiness and the enemy show up often together. Beware of the deceiver!

The Deceived

It might be easier to recognize the deceiver if we weren't surrounded by the deceived.

But when your friends, your family, and your favorite celebrity are all raving about this and posting pictures of that, it can feel agonizing to wear those old clothes, drive that old car, and eat dinner in your closed-concept kitchen. Add to that the millions of advertisements your eyes absorb each year, handcrafted to reach the visceral wants of your heart, and you have a struggle ahead of you.

Money, without a doubt, provides short-term pleasure, and our social media feeds are filled with the proof. She snaps a picture of her pedicured feet from the all-inclusive resort on the beach while his profile is blowing up with comments about his new boat. No one bothers to ask about anyone's credit card debt or stress levels or humility. We just see the pleasure—all the pros without concern for the cons.

Paul warned, "In [Christ] are hidden all the treasures of wisdom and knowledge. I tell you this so that no one may deceive you by fine-sounding arguments" (Colossians 2:3–4). Some arguments sound so good, good enough to deceive you, because the world has forgotten that the true treasure is found in Christ alone.

So in our always connected world, be careful the world doesn't deceive you too.

The Deceivable

The world wouldn't stand a chance of deceiving me if part of my heart wasn't so deceivable.

As much as I would love to consider myself a logical Christian, there is part of my heart that is primal, acting on instinct rather than intellect. Instead of sitting down with my prayed-over pros/cons chart, I too often make split-second decisions driven by emotions.

Part of me is like the ten-year-old trick-or-treater who showed up on author Jean Twenge's doorstep one Halloween. After Jean smiled and gave the kid two pieces of candy, he looked back at her and demanded, "More!"[3]

My sinful nature is like that. God gives me two blessings, but part of me wants a third. He gives me more than enough square footage, but part of me wants a few feet more. He gives me a car that runs, a shower that works, and more trips than a thousand impoverished kids will take combined, but part of me still, sadly, incessantly, wants more.

"The flesh desires what is contrary to the Spirit" (Galatians 5:17). Your flesh does too.

Which is why Jesus gave us a warning about the deceitfulness of wealth . . . and an answer.

The Answer to Wealth

Jesus' fruit-producing answer is not for us to avoid dollars but deception. When you open your spiritual eyes and realize what money is and what it isn't, what money gives and what it doesn't, how money blesses and how it curses, you are ready to embrace Agur's wisdom and, perhaps for the first time in your life, pray for "daily bread" and not a bottomless trust fund from above.

How do you get there? Personally, my greatest spiritual growth has happened in five specific ways.

1. Give/Save/Live

In my mid-20s, I heard a sermon by Pastor Andy Stanley—a guy with an unparalleled gift for crafting memorable ideas—where he summarized a wise way to handle money: Give/Save/Live. First, you give. Next, you save. Finally, you live off the rest.

Give/Save/Live, as Stanley teaches, opposes the "assumption that it is all for my consumption." By giving first, I am proving that I don't worship wealth. Money is not worthy of my heart, so I give it a demotion by donation and find joy in having 100% of God even if I'm living off less than 90% of my potential wealth.

This practice listens to Jesus say, "It is more blessed to give than to receive" (Acts 20:35) and responds with a hearty "Amen!" By not just receiving, I resist the enemy's deceiving.

When Kim and I had kids and got to the allowance phase of parenting, the first thing we did was pass on this sage advice to the next generation. To this day, our daughters have three jars on a bookshelf next to their beds.

Have you taken this step of faith yet? "Firstfruits giving," as some have traditionally called it, is an anti-deception act of discipleship, a God-given way to protect your heart from the thorns of greed. I won't tell you how much to give or to whom to give it, but I pray that you would first give.

Just like God gave his first and best for you.

2. Research Rich People

This might make me a total creeper, but I love to watch people. Not like "watch from the tree outside their bedroom with the binoculars I got off Amazon," but watch how happy people are who have more than I have.

One of the benefits of our oversharing culture is that it only takes a glance at a celebrity's Instagram account or a few minutes of a recent interview to realize how loving, peaceful, and joy-filled rich people are. Google the song lyrics of the latest pop star, reading each line and also between them. Be dazzled by the clothes and the cars, the mansions and the world tours, but then ask yourself, "How happy are they, really?"

What I have seen, time and time again, from lottery winners to social media influencers, is that more money doesn't mean more rest, more safety, or more contentment. God has given us experiential evidence to protect us from the deceitfulness of wealth.

Or, if you're not good with Google, just listen to Isaiah: "Why spend money on what is not bread, and your labor on what does not satisfy?" (Isaiah 55:2).

There is only one thing that satisfies your soul, and you can't labor for enough money to buy it. It's free and all yours through faith in Jesus Christ.

3. Question the Joneses

Keeping up with the Joneses is the best way to keep busy. That's why, instead of trying to imitate my wealthiest neighbors, I question them.

When our family drives past a fancy neighborhood, the one with the three-car garages and the two-story windows, I comment, "That's a lot of vacuuming." Glancing back at my daughters, I'll ask them, "Seriously, how much time do you think it takes to vacuum in there?"

Okay, it's a dumb thing to say, but I'm trying to engage their minds and not just their eyes. My hope is that they'll start to think of the downsides of wealth, of the cost of bigger/taller/more spacious, of what families like that might have to sacrifice in order to live in homes like that. How much time do their chores take? How much do they pay in property taxes? How often do their security systems go off during the year?

There are, indeed, wonderful blessings to big homes, nice boats, and fast cars, and I am grateful to the generous, hospitable, and kingdom-building wealthy folks whom I know. But there are also blessings to living in 1,000 square feet, driving a used car, and wearing the same clothes until they wear out. Such lifestyles provide us space in our schedules and in our minds to meditate on the Word, spontaneously serve those in need, and take a nap as we enjoy the true rest we find in Christ.

So question the Joneses. They look stressed, don't they?

4. Prioritize and Protect

Have you seen the classic illustration of the jar, the rocks, the pebbles, the sand, and the water?

YouTube can explain it way better than I can, but the gist is that for everything to fit, you need to start with the rocks first. Get it backward, and it won't quite work. In the same way, life only fits together when you start with the big things first.

We might say the deeply sanctified start with the right spacing. If you give the Word the margin it needs to grow, the time required for meditation and obedience, you'll quickly run out of space in your schedule, forcing you to say no to what you might have earlier said yes to.

For example, I have found that loving my wife works best when I take her on a date every Friday night. I could have a crazy schedule from Sunday through Thursday where we don't get much quality time, but if I can protect our Friday nights, Kim and I both end up feeling loved, respected, and close.

I plant a "love your wife" seed and give it space to grow.*

What would protecting priorities look like in your life? Perhaps you are single and have the margin in your week to serve like Jesus served, giving your time to mentor a middle-school student or serve on the board of a nonprofit in your city. You could, of course, get another job or pick up another shift, but maybe your priority will be serving a cause that fits with your passion. Or maybe your parents are older, requiring more of your time and attention than they ever have before. Buying a cabin or pulling the trigger on a boat wouldn't be sinful, but it could clutter your schedule and prevent you from showing them kindness in the final season of their lives. Or perhaps you have enough savings to stay in your three-bedroom house, even after the kids are grown. But downsizing would give you more margin in your bank account and on your weekends to support the homeless shelter in town.

These are suggestions, not commands, but I hope they encourage you to think first of fruit, of love and goodness and faithfulness. Put those "rocks" into your life first, and you'll quickly figure out what fits and what doesn't.

---

* By that, I technically mean "love *my* wife." Me loving your wife, if you are a married man, would be both sinful and a quick way to your one-star Amazon review.

5. Meditate on Jesus

The best way to resist the allure of wealth is Jesus. I have saved this point for the end of this list not because it is the fifth most important way to guard yourself against the love of money, but rather because I want the last thing in your mind to be the name of Jesus.

A restless heart is easy prey for any good-intentioned marketer or ill-intentioned devil. But a heart that rests in Jesus, that breathes deeply and inhales his never-ending supply of love, has Sherlock-esque sense against the deceiver and his tricks.

Christ invites you: "Come to me, all you who are weary and burdened, and I will give you rest" (Matthew 11:28). Jesus' rest isn't found in a Sleep Number mattress but in his mercy, in his willingness to love you despite your flaws and smile at you despite your sins.

Notice his invitation: "Come." He isn't pushing you away or waiting until you prove your worth to him. He wants you to come right now.

Notice what he is offering: "Come to me." Jesus wants to give you himself, a Savior who has a long history of loving the most unlikely people. Others in your life might not invite you to their table because of your past, but Jesus will. Jesus is.

Notice who is included in the invitation: "Come to me, all you . . ." Not some of you. Not the top 20 of you. All of you. You might have a terabyte of evidence that you are unworthy to step into Jesus' presence, but our Lord is inviting you all the same.

Finally, notice the type of people who need this invitation: "Come to me, all you who are weary and burdened . . ." Maybe the truths of this chapter have burdened your conscience, reminding you of paychecks you chased after and financial goals you pursued at the expense of your own spiritual maturity. You are the very type of person whom Jesus is inviting to a better life, an abundant life that isn't based on the abundance of your possessions but instead on the abundance of his love.

In his desire to give this kind of rest to your soul, Jesus entered this world and was not deceived, not even by the deceiver himself. When riches could have bought needed bread and a comfortable bed, Jesus rejected the offer and turned to his Father, growing and maturing so he could bear the fruit of salvation years later. Although the Lord could have kept every shekel for himself, he instead paid taxes, gave to the poor, and brought his own offerings to the temple, assuring the world that wealth was not required to live a life of joy.

Paul talked about this aspect of Jesus' work when he said, "Though he was rich, yet for your sake he became poor, so that you through his poverty might become rich" (2 Corinthians 8:9).

Through Jesus, who died without ever owning a home on the seashores of Galilee, you and I have become rich. Our spiritual accounts are filled with the gold coins of God's grace, spilling out, covering over our sins, and assuring us that our future is secure as long as Jesus is around.

When the next internet ad scratches at your heart, meditate on the One who came "that they may have life, and have it to the full" (John 10:10). If every spiritual gift is already yours through faith in Jesus, then anything wealth can offer you is small and temporary by comparison. When this reality sinks deep into your soul, the thorns wither and the fruit of true joy starts to ripen.

You are loved, right now, because of Jesus. You matter, already, because of Jesus. You have an eternity of experiences awaiting you, guaranteed, because of Jesus.

> You who have no money, come, buy and eat! Come, buy wine and milk without money and without cost. Why spend money on what is not bread, and your labor on what does not satisfy?

Listen, listen to me, and eat what is good, and you will delight in the richest of fare. Give ear and come to me; listen, that you may live. I will make an everlasting covenant with you, my faithful love.

Isaiah 55:1–3

Do you remember my friend who helped close multimillion-dollar deals but was struggling to find rest? I asked him how he overcame those challenges, and he shared, "It was always when I started my day with Jesus. . . . Too often I'd want to dive into my to-do list versus first starting it with Jesus at the top. Days I did were so much better, and they still are!"

He is right. So let the world run after temporary things. You already have something better through Jesus.

STUDY QUESTIONS

1. Jesus listed both the worries of life and the deceitfulness of wealth as having the same effect on our hearts, that is, choking out the Word. What do worry and wealth have in common? What differences do you see between them?

2. Reflect on your own life story in regard to money. In what ways has making more money blessed you? In what ways has it complicated your life?

3. Soak in the words of 1 Timothy 6:6–16. As you read, jot down at least ten insights that you find in Paul's expansive teaching on the topic of money.

4. Schedule a time to talk with someone who appears to make/have more money than you. Gently ask them about their joys, stresses, and schedule. As you listen, keep your ears open for how their levels of joy, peace, and contentment compare to your own.

5. King Solomon once wrote, "Those who trust in their riches will fall, but the righteous will thrive like a green leaf" (Proverbs 11:28). What does it mean to "trust in" riches as opposed to just having riches? How does being righteous (right with God and seeking to do the right thing) provide a thriving life no matter what tax bracket you are in?

6. Which of the five suggestions at the end of this chapter intrigues you the most? What would be different about next week if you put it into practice?

7

Wanting

> The seed that fell among thorns stands for those who hear, but as they go on their way they are choked by life's worries, riches and *pleasures*, and they do not mature . . . Still others, like seed sown among thorns, hear the word; but the worries of this life, the deceitfulness of wealth and *the desires for other things* come in and choke the word, making it unfruitful.
>
> Mark 4; Luke 8, selected verses (emphasis mine)

The Screen Seduced Me

Since I highly value transparency, I need to confess to you what I do at night.

After years of self-control, I have found myself back in a bad habit. When my kids are in bed and my wife is asleep, I creep down into the basement, close the door behind me, turn on the TV, and drop the volume low enough that no one can hear. And there, alone, I get lost in the soft glow of the screen. An hour passes, then two, sometimes, shamefully, even three, before I trudge my way back up the stairs, crawl into bed next to the woman I vowed to love, and wonder why I keep going back . . .

. . . to Zelda.*

Technically, there is nothing sinful about a 40-year-old man spending hours of his evenings venturing through the kingdom of Hyrule in search of magical swords and armor-increasing elixirs before the evil Ganon regains control of the land.† However, when I step back and do the math of my recent gaming habits, something inside of me questions the return on the investment, wondering what else I could have done with my life if I had passed on purchasing that Nintendo Switch.

You might not be a gamer, but you face the same dilemma, namely, filling your life with not-exactly-wrong things that don't produce the things that God loves most.

Which is exactly what Jesus warned about in his parable.

The Desires for Other Things

Unlike the more obvious evils of worry and the deceitfulness of money, the last part of Jesus' description of the thorny soil is seemingly innocent. "The desires for other things come in and choke the word, making it unfruitful" (Mark 4:19).

"Other things." Not evil things. Not sinful things. Not destructive things. Just "other things." On Jesus' Top 6 Threats list is the seemingly harmless category "other things."

In Luke's version of the story, Jesus reduces the phrase down to *pleasures*, a word that simply means stuff that makes you happy, such as entertainment, hobbies, and the things you love to do after the workday is over. A surprising addition to Jesus' list, don't you think?

---

* This section is shamelessly clickbait-y, but I couldn't resist.
† Sharing that last sentence on a dating site would compel most women to swipe left. Kim, don't you go dying on me!

If you like fancy words, this is what some call *adiaphora.**
Adiaphora comes from a Greek word that means "does not de-
stroy," a concept that some theologians use for all the things in
life that God neither commands nor forbids. We have freedom
to do them or not do them.†

Should Christians sing classic hymns or contemporary songs
in church? Adiaphora. Should you work 30 hours a week at
your job or 40 or 50? Adiaphora. Does God want Christians to
go to college? Adiaphora. Must believers love sausage breakfast
sandwiches? Logically, yes. But, technically, that's adiaphora
too.

In other words, adiaphora are all those things that don't have
a "you shall" or "you shall not" attached to them. God hasn't
given a thumbs-up or a thumbs-down, so you have the personal
freedom to make your own choice.

But, according to Jesus, choose wisely.

Because sometimes "other things" can get in the way of
the best things. Jesus says, "They are choked by life's worries, riches and pleasures, and they do not mature. . . . The
desires for other things come in and choke the word, making it unfruitful" (Luke 8:14; Mark 4:19). *Immature* and
unfruitful—two descriptions of too many of us within the
Christian church.

We have talked about how worries can make you sinfully
busy and how money can deceive you into an overbooked life,
so let's focus on how some of the more innocent things can
have the same effect on your faith. We could apply this in a
hundred different ways, but I am going to focus on four that
most threaten my faith and the faith of other followers of Jesus
at my church:

---

* Apparently, my word processor doesn't call it that, because I just got scolded
by the red line for misspelled words.
† The German word for *adiaphora* is *Mittledinge*, which I challenge you to say
in a German accent without giggling.

Shows. Sports. Apps. News.

Shows

If you haven't felt depressed in a while, go to the website tiii.me. The minimalist home page will ask you to do one simple thing and promises to give you one simple reply.

The simple thing? You type in a TV series that you have seen, in part or in its entirety.

The simple reply? It tells you how many hours and minutes you spent watching it.

Seriously, you don't want to do this. I learned that I have spent nearly 47 hours with Walter White and *Breaking Bad*, 72 hours enduring/enjoying Michael Scott's awkwardness on *The Office*, and 114 hours watching the undead chase the living on *The Walking Dead*.*

If you don't feel bad about your very existence just yet, do you know how much time it would take you to read the Bible? If you're an average reader, you could read all four biographies of Jesus' life—Matthew and Mark and Luke and John—in around 8 hours. Spend another 9 and you could finish the New Testament. The entire Bible, that massive book that few of us have time to read from cover to cover, would take 74 hours and 28 minutes.

Or 12 minutes per day in the course of one year.

That means most fans of *The Office* could have read the entire Bible in just a couple hours more time than they spent watching the series. *Walking Dead* Heads could have become experts in the actual resurrection of the dead by reading the gospels 14 times! Honestly, I don't want to look at my Netflix queue and recall all the other series I binged and forgot about. . . .

Is Jesus against streaming entertainment? No. I happen to think that Jesus loves that *Office* episode where Jim suspended

---

* At least I didn't waste 98 hours and 20 minutes with Ross and Rachel like my wife did binging *Friends*.

Dwight's stapler in Jell-O. But the point from Jesus' parable isn't that we need to watch out for "evil things." His point is that we need to beware of "other things."

Wonder with me for a minute—what would our lives look like with less "other things" and more fruitful things? If I could somehow travel back in time, unsee that series, and reinvest those one hundred hours in something else, something better, what impact would I make? Would I regret the reallocation of my limited time?

Imagine if you had spent just ten of those hours writing thank-you cards to the people whom God used to bless you during your life. Handwritten, snail-mailed, opened, I guarantee, before anything else that was stuffed in the mailbox that day. I guarantee that your words would not be speed-read but instead kept somewhere special, tucked in a journal or magnetized to a fridge.

Or imagine how much joy your mother would experience if you spent a percentage of those one hundred hours calling her, listening to her, and sharing your life with her, even though you aren't her little baby anymore. That act of goodness would stand out in a world of parents who are aching for a continued connection with their kids.

Or how affair-proof would marriages be if every couple spent one hundred hours serving each another, praying for each other, and speaking their spouse's love language? Quality love takes quantity time, and cutting back on a single series could provide just that. Netflixing and chilling can have relational benefits too,* but couples who get in the habit of inviting a screen into most of their private moments end up missing out on a greater blessing.

Maybe the website that calculates the hours and minutes isn't depressing. Maybe it's a wake-up call to a church that has

---

* If you don't know what that means, ask a young person you know.

been caught up in culture's trance, believing that we *need* these "other things" to relax, to unwind, to be happy.

Maybe Jesus wants something better.

Here's a place for you to start: Crunch the numbers. Go back to your chart from a previous chapter and figure out how much time you spend streaming movies, watching shows, and getting lost in a digital spiral of YouTube videos. Compare your data to other things in your life—face-to-face time with friends, prayer, volunteering—and then share your findings with someone who loves you and loves God.

I have a hunch that you might rethink your relationship with "other things."

Sports

I heart sports so much. In grade school, I played soccer and basketball and ping-pong. In high school, I added ice hockey, roller hockey, and tennis. In my 20s, I added distance running and hip-hop dancing.* Put on an NFL, NHL, or EPL game, and I'll start to care about teams that I know nothing about.

The other day, however, my youngest daughter made a valid observation about sports. "Daddy, football games are so long."

I suppose she had a point. Three hours of watching strangers chase each other around a big rectangle is a significant investment for those of us who live within space and time. God might be able to multitask while he keeps an eye on the latest season, but we mortals have to pick and choose what gets our attention in any given moment.

My hometown team, the Green Bay Packers, has a recent history of making it to the playoffs, meaning that we get 17+ games each year. At three hours each, the games fill every fall with more hours of screen time than some Packer fans will

---

* I can do a single break dancing move, which all the kids love at weddings. However, at my age, my brittle hips are a relevant concern.

spend working out or having meaningful conversations with their own children.

In addition, some of us who love the Green and Gold don't just watch the games. We watch the preseason interviews, the pregame show, and the postgame analysis. Add the midweek radio show, the coach's reaction to last week's matchup, and the upcoming draft, and you have as many hours as it takes to watch all of *Grey's Anatomy.**

Please don't hear me hating on your favorite pastimes or your Sunday screen time. If Jesus opposed sports, he had every chance to drop a "you shall not watch people run" into his teaching. He didn't, which means you and I have the freedom to enjoy a good game.

Once again, however, Jesus' concern is for something greater. He knows how "other things," such as being a faithful fan, can prevent your faith from reaching maturity.

A few years ago, a school near our church asked for some help with mentoring. Since my schedule is flexible during the school day, I offered to help out for 30 minutes each week, playing basketball with a few fourth graders and attempting to be a positive influence in their lives.

That's not a Mother Teresa act of selflessness, mind you. It was once a week for the time it takes some of us to shower, shave, and eat a Pop-Tart.

What I didn't expect, however, was how much blessing God could bring out of half an hour. After a few weeks, I got to know not only the young man I was mentoring but also his classmates, his teachers, and the staff at his school. Even more important, when things were hard at home—as they often were for many students at this school where 50% live on the verge of homelessness—getting out of class to play H-O-R-S-E was a bright spot in the lives of these precious kids.

---

* A whopping 276 hours!

That all happened in 30 minutes a week. One-sixth of a single NFL game.

When I consider the impact that half an hour of love can make, I start to rethink my love for sports. They are good, but I have experienced things that are greater.

Haven't you? As you look back on your own life, haven't you forgotten nearly all the matches, while remembering so many of those moments when you served, gave, and loved?

That's the fruit that Jesus is talking about!

If you are a big sports fan, here are two suggestions: You could step away entirely or you could become a "one and done" fan.

While stepping away entirely might seem absurd and undoable, those who have taken this radical step would disagree. When I cut my cable and gave up SportsCenter, I thought I would be miserable. I wasn't. In no time, I adjusted to my new normal and had an extra hour in my day. Similarly, after a few years of Mexican soccer addiction, I quit cold turkey and my life is still worth living.

What if—I'm being bold here—you gave up watching sports for three months? What if you conducted a grand experiment on your own heart, swapping out "other things" for other things like offering to help a neighbor with a home remodel project or asking the principal at the local elementary school if there's anything you can do to help your community?

I am not asking you to never watch sports again. But you might just find that loving people well brings you more joy than all those hours yelling at your big screen.

If giving up sports for three months feels impossible, what about a 30-day trial of "one and done"? Pick one game per week, give your full attention to a few hours of athletic drama, and call it done for the next seven days. This practice will force you to be picky and only allow the best matchups to be worthy of your time.

With those extra hours, you could read the gospels, deepen

an important friendship, reach out to someone who recently lost their spouse, or start a prayer journal for the first time in your life.

Just so I'm clear: sports aren't sinful, and watching one game, two games, or four games isn't inherently forbidden. But Jesus is urging us to think about maximum maturity and above-average fruitfulness. With God's help, that could describe you and me.

> Be very careful, then, how you live—not as unwise but as wise.
>
> Ephesians 5:15

Apps

True confession—I open my apps before I open my Bible.

According to approximately 38 podcasters I've heard, it is essential to fill my mind with God's Word before I let the drama of the day's headlines get into my headspace. But, out of habit and not defiance, I wake up, empty my bladder, and scroll on my phone before opening my Bible.

There's the weather app, my calendar app, the podcasting app, *USA Today*'s app for the news, Strides for my goals, and, of course, an app to check my email. And, apparently, all that app time adds up.

That's what my phone told me. A few years ago, Apple decided to crush all our spirits by adding a simple feature called Screen Time. With a quick click, you can now see exactly how much time you spend on your phone each day. It even breaks down your usage of each individual app.

Last week, unless Apple is exaggerating, I averaged 1 hour and 20 minutes on my phone each day, which adds up to 9 hours and 20 minutes of phone time for the week. And this doesn't include my Zelda-filled evenings or the Netflix I watch when I'm snuggled up next to Kim. And I thought I was good at managing my screen time.

Ah, facts!

I probably don't have to repeat myself, but I'm not hating on the folks who create apps or the social media gurus who keep us connected to friends and family. I'm just wondering how I might have grown had I been more intentional with "other things."

Or, to stick with Jesus' metaphor, I'm wondering what I might have grown.

As a father, I have noticed that my kids crave one thing more than all the other things in the world—my full attention. I could buy them a Switch or get them a puppy, but what fills up their hearts unlike anything else is having all of me. When I listen to their stories, looking them in the eye, and join them in their projects with phone-free hands, they float with joy.

That fort we made in the living room with every pillow, chair, and blanket under our roof. The date at the coffee shop where we sketched characters from her new art book. The random games we invented, such as the one where I chase the children with ping-pong balls and try my best to "sting" them with a full-force swing.*

Honestly, app-checking seems so unworthy when I recall those memories. The fruit of goodness, kindness, and joy taste so much better than the digital bites the internet offers.

Have you tasted and seen the same? What good could you do with those extra minutes? What rest could you reach with an hour away from the enticing rectangular glow? What other things could you enjoy if you weren't so busy with "other things"?

News

Maybe it was just 2020. At the end of an exhausting year figuring out and fighting the pandemic, America came to another election, but this didn't feel like another election.

While politics have always been partisan, this time the hatred

---

* We call it Stinger Ball, and no game is as requested by my kids, niece, and nephew. Someone always gets hurt, but everyone always ends up happy (and rather sweaty).

was hard to hide. Members of our church, otherwise level-headed people, were overcome by anger, fear, and petty name-calling. Our pastoral team had to get used to lengthy tirades from both sides, Christians accusing us of poor shepherding for not condemning "those people," the ones who had just chastised us for not being more direct with "those people."

At one point, I asked my wife, "Do you know anyone who is both deeply political and impressively fruitful?" She stared at me blankly. I gave her the same look.

Maybe my sample size is too small, but I am concerned that what we call "news" today is actually a storm that is stripping the unripened fruit off of the trees we call Christians. With a good Father, a perfect Savior, and an empowering Spirit, we Christians have the potential to produce peace that would make the world drool with envy. An unbelieving culture could marvel, like it did in the early church, "Look how they love one another!"

But I don't think we are there. Scratch that. I know we are not there.

A former professor once said, "You are what you read." Spend enough time with that author, and you will likely absorb her message and imitate her tone. That idea inspires me, reminding me that the Good Book and other good books have the potential to shape me into the image of Jesus, making my life look more and more like his. But that quote terrifies me too, warning me that other media messages can have the same effect.

While my knowledge of media and marketing is shallow, I do know that fear, anger, and exaggeration set people apart. When there are hundreds of channels, millions of podcasts, and billions of websites, those that tap into our deepest fears and stoke our strongest anger will get our attention, our views, our clicks, and the ad dollars that encourage the hosts to stay angry.

So can I ask you news lovers and political junkies to do some self-reflection and ask, "Am I fruitful?" You might be right, patriotic, or woke. But are you fruitful? Would your social media friends consider you good, kind, patient, gentle, loving, and peacemaking not just to "your people" but to all people?

If not, beware. Your desire for "other things" might choke out the powerful words you heard the last time you sat in church or opened your Bible.

> Be completely humble and gentle; be patient, bearing with one another in love. Make every effort to keep the unity of the Spirit through the bond of peace.
>
> Ephesians 4:2–3

Patience. Love. Peace. That's the good fruit that comes when your heart isn't busy paying attention to "other things."

Desire + Knowledge = Good

King Solomon once warned, "Desire without knowledge is not good" (Proverbs 19:2). Desiring, wanting, and seeking without stopping for knowledge is not a good way to become wise.

My goal in exploring the "other things" in Jesus' story is not to slap a "foolish!" label on your favorite pastimes but to help you step back and think about whether a good thing (like shows, sports, apps, and news) might be preventing a better thing (like love, joy, and peace).

I have tried not to add or subtract from God's will, commanding what he hasn't or forbidding what he didn't, but I have tried to get you to dream. What could happen if . . . ? Who would be blessed when . . . ? What kind of Christian would you become if only . . . ?

If you picked up this book, I bet you desire to seek God first, to love people well, and to live life to your fullest potential. I desire that too, which is why the painful pricks of this chapter are good work, a necessary step to clearing out the soil and waiting for God to grow something better for our future.

Better Desires, Better Things

In 1972 Johnny Cash stepped onto the stage of Dallas's Cotton Bowl in front of a crowd that swelled to 150,000 people who were drawn to Jesus. The act was part of the Explo '72 Conference, which was organized by Billy Graham and Bill Bright, the founder of Campus Crusade for Christ.

Cash told the massive crowd, "I have tried drugs and a little of everything else, and there is nothing in the world more satisfying than having the kingdom of God building inside of you and growing."[1]

Notice Johnny's point. In Jesus, he had found a satisfying joy that this world could not match. To be specific, Mr. Cash mentioned that neither "drugs" nor "everything else" could offer him what King Jesus did through his Word.

I like that. It's easy (or easier) for Christians to see that Christ is better than drugs. However, it takes ears to hear to realize that Christ is also better than "everything else," than the "other things" that we could do without the Father's condemnation.

Will it be hard to change our habits? For sure. Will we miss the thrill of another fourth-quarter comeback or the satisfying ending of the latest streaming series? Probably. Will there be painful moments in our pursuit of a countercultural life? Yes, and some will be as painful as ripping out a clump of thorns in your garden.

But will it be worth it? Ask the young woman who volunteers at the crisis center even though she is out of touch with the latest shows. Ask the father who turns off the TV to be tummy-down on the carpet as his baby girl learns to crawl. Ask the family at grandma's funeral if her kindness and generosity were a waste of her limited time.

There are some things that are better things than other things.

So how could your desire for a better life lead you to better things? As you consider your screen time, your relationship to sports, your app usage, and your commitment to the daily news, where could you say no so that God's seed could produce more fruit?

Or, as I've found more helpful, where could you prioritize "yes" so that "other things" end up unable to fit in your schedule? Would blocking out 30 minutes every morning for Bible study and prayer force you to limit your scroll between wake-up and work? Would volunteering once a week force you to put away your phone and give your full attention to a cause that could use your help?

I am not sure which good works God has planned for you to do personally, but I do know that good works are indeed good. They are better than other things.

Author Scott Sauls tells the story of the time that U2 front man and philanthropist Bono got shot down by a pastor. Bono had been reading the works of pastor Eugene Peterson and wanted to meet the man himself. Peterson, at the time, was working on *The Message*, his personal paraphrase of the Bible, and was deep into turning the prophet Isaiah's words into modern English. Due to the intensity of the work, Peterson politely passed on Bono's offer to get together and talk.

Later, after the two had met and become friends, a journalist asked Peterson to justify his refusal to meet one of the most famous humans on the planet. He exclaimed, "This is *Bono* we're talking about, for goodness' sakes!"

But Peterson gently smiled and explained, "But this is *Isaiah* we're talking about."[2]

There's something better than Bono. Someone better. Because Isaiah was pointing to Immanuel, the God who would be with us, to Jesus.

Maybe that's the right way to think about this part of Jesus' parable. The world, baffled, exclaims, "This is *the Super Bowl* we are talking about. And *the Senate* that is at stake. And the series finale of *the best show ever*!"

But we can gently smile and explain, "But this is *Jesus* we're talking about."

When I studied everything the Bible had to say about desire, I was reminded why Jesus is worthy of plenty of space in our hearts.

Although there was "nothing in his appearance that we should desire him," something about his character drew us toward him (Isaiah 53:2). Jesus must not have had gorgeous eyes or high cheekbones, but he possessed a beauty that age could not touch. His integrity made it safe for women, children, and broken people to approach him without the fear that he would use them for his own advantage.

Since "what a person desires is unfailing love," we came to see Jesus as "what is desired by all nations," the only true source of continual, constant, and reliable love (Proverbs 19:22; Haggai 2:7). Others would inevitably fail us, but not Jesus. Never Jesus. Day after day, we could drag our suitcase full of failures to the foot of the cross, knowing that his love would never run out and his compassion would never dry up.

We have tasted and seen enough of the Lord's goodness to confess, "Earth has nothing I desire besides you" and "Your name and renown are the desire of our hearts" (Psalm 73:25; Isaiah 26:8). While we might think that we need another show, another episode, another playoff game, or another way to entertain ourselves, what we know is that our hearts desire things that last. Therefore, our desires are actually for the eternal God, the Father who offers us eternal life in the name of the One who has been his Son from eternity past.

We love this Jesus because he is the only one who walked into this cluttered world with the simple passion that said, "I have come to do your will, my God" (Hebrews 10:7). And then he did. He did everything the Father asked of him, earning nothing but the proud smile of his Abba in heaven, an expression that Jesus gifted to us when he exchanged our sinfulness for his righteousness. Our deep desire for a Father who sees us, knows us, and likes us is satisfied once and for all.

Only Jesus is that good. This is why Jesus is our greatest passion. Sports and shows are good, but only God is great.

Take delight in the LORD, and he will give you the desires of your heart.

Psalm 37:4

STUDY QUESTIONS

1. In Jesus' day, there were no shows, few sports, no apps, and slow-to-arrive news. What "other things" do you suppose were threats for Christians in that generation? List at least three.

2. Ecclesiastes 6:2 says, "God gives some people wealth, possessions and honor, so that they lack nothing their hearts desire, but God does not grant them the ability to enjoy them, and strangers enjoy them instead. This is meaningless, a grievous evil." What do these words add to the big ideas of this chapter?

3. Brainstorm ten "fruitful" things you could do for your neighbors, your family, or your community if you had

two extra hours to spare each week. Which of those ten things excites you the most? Pray that God would give you the wisdom to manage your time well so that you can give others a glimpse of his unfailing love.

4. Evaluate this statement: People change most when what they want most changes.

5. Paul once confessed, "Whatever were gains to me I now consider loss for the sake of Christ" (Philippians 3:7). How does a glorious, exalted view of Jesus change your perspective on what truly matters in life? In what ways have you seen this already in your faith journey? How could meditating on the heart of Jesus (by reading Hebrews, for example) decrease your desire for "other things"?

6. Who is someone whom you consider, to use Jesus' word from Luke 8, "mature" in their faith? Reach out to them and ask about how they spend their free time, noting their relationship to shows, sports, apps, and news. If their example inspires you, "Consider the outcome of their way of life and imitate their faith" (Hebrews 13:7).

8

Not Waiting

A farmer went out to sow his seed. As he was scattering the seed, some fell along the path, and the birds came and ate it up. Some fell on rocky places, where it did not have much soil. It sprang up quickly, because the soil was shallow. But when the sun came up, the plants were scorched, and they withered because they had no root. Other seed fell among thorns, which grew up and choked the plants. Still other seed fell on good soil, where it produced a crop—a hundred, sixty or thirty times what was sown.

Matthew 13:3–8

The Essential Thing Jesus Implied

When you started to study this parable from Jesus, you might have questioned the outline of this book. Reading through Matthew, Mark, and Luke, it's fairly easy to see five threats to the farmer's seed. So you might have thought, where is the sixth?

After thanking you for paying such close attention to the Word, I would open my Bible, run my finger along the lines, and read aloud, "A farmer went out to sow his SEED. As he was scattering the SEED, some fell along the path, and the birds came and ate it up. Some fell on rocky places, where it did not have much soil. It sprang up quickly, because the soil was shallow. But when the sun came up, the plants were scorched, and they withered because they had no root. Other SEED fell among thorns, which grew up and choked the plants. Still other SEED fell on good soil, where it produced a crop—a hundred, sixty or thirty times what was sown" (Matthew 13:3–8).

And then I would Google "How long do seeds take to grow?" or "Sowing to harvest timeline" or "Best Poppin John dance videos."* Then, the internet would remind us that every seed has this in common: waiting. Not just a few seconds or a few minutes or a few days but a few months, if not more.

That's why farmers don't sow after breakfast and harvest before lunch. They wait and wait and wait, spending weeks checking the weather, watering their fields, and praying for plenty of sun. Likewise, every recreational gardener plants onions and cilantro and jalapeños in hopes of making salsa sometime later, long after the seeds were first placed in the ground.

If you didn't understand the nature of seeds, you would get frustrated by the process, wouldn't you? You follow the directions exactly, digging to the precise depth and spacing out the seeds at the perfect distance, but nothing happens. So you set up the sprinkler, dialing it to the gentle rain setting, but nothing happens. So you give it a chance to enjoy a cloudless, sun-filled day, but all you get is more of nothing.

Just a patch of brown and a wasted day of work.

But obviously, we know better. We know the science of how seeds work, so we adjust our expectations, put in the work, and protect our potential fruit from all the dangers that it will

---

* I have a personal rule that every third Google search has to be for Poppin John, the best moonwalker on earth.

face in the upcoming months. Because vine-ripened tomatoes, mint that you scratch-and-sniff on your fingers, and fresh corn that you will bathe in butter and salt are well worth the wait.

These are the same expectations we have with children. The little ones we love didn't start little. They started microscopically, entering this world without even being noticed. What couple has ever made love, rolled over, and said, "We're pregnant!"?

The moment Goliath was conceived, his parents didn't have a clue. Neither did yours. All those feet and inches that we call *you* came not only from minuscule origins but also from a long, long, long waiting period. It took a few weeks for your mom to even know she was pregnant. You didn't show up as a baby bump until two or three months after that. Your first breath was, on average, nine months after your conception, the time it takes to start and end seventh grade.

My point is that your parents, like local farmers, had to wait to see if their "seed" had produced anything at all.

But the waiting game was far from over. For the next two decades, your mom and dad likely fed you, bathed you, and tried their best not to kill you. They expended countless calories running around to keep you alive, educated, and on track to be a functional adult. Yet they rarely noticed when you grew. It took your uncle, on his annual visit during Christmas, to say, "Look how big he is!" or friends from the last place you lived to say, "I cannot believe how much she's grown." Time teaches us that things grow, but they rarely grow in ways that we see.

This is a reality that you must not forget. You can, with God's Word, grow in wonderful ways, but you will, by God's plan, have to wait.

Worship and Wait

Jesus' choice to call God's Word a "seed" is his not-so-subtle reminder that we must wait. While God can (and generously does) produce peace while we hear the gospel preached and joy while we sing of Jesus' unfailing love, the best fruit won't show up for a while.

But the Word is working, even while you are waiting.

In Psalm 1, the opening song in this Old Testament set list, the author describes a blessed person like this:

> Blessed is the one . . . whose delight is in the law of the LORD, and who meditates on his law day and night. That person is like a tree planted by streams of water, which yields its fruit in season and whose leaf does not wither—whatever they do prospers.
>
> Psalm 1:1–3

Blessed. Yielding fruit. Prospering while others wither. There's the potential we have been pursuing in the pages of this book.

But notice the details—"Day and night . . . like a tree . . . in season." Part of me wishes the psalmist said, "Blessed is the one whose faith is like a microwave dinner, which goes from frozen to fantastic in 2 minutes and 45 seconds." But it doesn't say that. (Not even in the original Hebrew.)

There is a blessed life that God's Word offers, but that blessed life is miles down Waiting Drive. And the speed limit is 25 miles per hour.

This shouldn't shock anyone who has read the Bible. God's promise about Abraham and Sarah's exponential potential—descendants like the stars in the sky—took 25 years of waiting to add just one baby. God's oath to give Israel the land east of the Mediterranean Sea wasn't fulfilled until Joshua crossed the Jordan six hundred years later. God's plans for the exiles of Israel to prosper, famously written in Jeremiah 29:11, took a solid 70 years to bear good fruit.

And don't even get me started on Jesus! God told the devil that a seed of the woman would come to crush the head of sin and death, and however old the human race is, it was a long time before Mary pushed Jesus out! Isaiah's prophecy of a virgin being with child was seven centuries before there was no room in Bethlehem's inn, and Malachi's message, "He's coming!" was about as far back from Christ's birth as the Pilgrims are from modern Americans.

Bible readers, of all people, should know that God does great things after long waits. He's a seed-sowing, patiently waiting kind of Father.

His wiser children try not to fall too far from the Father's tree.

We Hate the Wait

Despite the logic of gardens, our experience with babies, and the Old Testament stories, the fact remains that 99.9% of us hate the wait.*

That's why I bought a new TV last Christmas. My old TV, a gift from my brother, required a two-minute warm-up before it would work, like that really old guy who goes to the YMCA and stretches before stepping on the treadmill. The TV would immediately power on but then say "preparing" and refuse to acknowledge our impatient desire to get started on our latest show.

Two minutes! That might not have felt like much to Moses, but this isn't the Bronze Age. We Americans enjoy our dinner slow cooked, but we plan to pick it up as fast food.

If you consider yourself a patient person, here's a test of your waiting muscles—watch an old movie. Cuddle up on the couch and stream the original 1964 version of *Mary Poppins*, for example. Because you will be immediately confronted with 2 minutes and 59 seconds of front-end credits.

---

* .1% of the population is called Waitophiles, weirdos who love driving in school zones and streaming videos on terrible Wi-Fi.

I'm not joking. Two minutes and fifty-nine real-life seconds of just credits. If you can get through it without checking your phone, I will give you a trillion dollars.

Before you get to the first song, the first dance number, or the first minutely interesting part of the plot, you will be forced to read who styled everyone's hair, edited the sound, and designed the nursery sequence.* Within three minutes, a modern movie would have had three explosions, two sex scenes, and a cameo from Samuel L. Jackson.

Oh, the times have been a-changin', and those changes have been hard on waiting.

Despite my preference for post-movie credits, these cultural changes have challenged the Christian faith in subtle but powerful ways. If God's Word is like a seed that takes time to grow, what happens when people don't have the capacity to wait? What are the spiritual implications of a generation that can't imagine investing months of their lives into something that appears not to have produced any noticeable changes?

What would happen to a garden whose gardener gave up three weeks after planting the seed?

Jesus' word choice is a challenge to fast-paced people of faith. We will end up immature and unfruitful unless we adjust our expectations and become like farmers and parents, believing that the best things will take months to grow.

But the wait will be worth it.

Dimmer Switches and Snooze Bars

If your brain can handle a change in metaphors, think of waiting for the seed like a dimmer switch.

A light switch is a quick click between extremes, from total darkness to 100-watt light in a fraction of a second. This, of

---

* I'm not making those titles up. I watched all 2:59 of the credits. And nearly died.

course, is what all of us would prefer from God, a one-passage click to restore a strained friendship, to transform an anxious teen into a no-fear disciple, and to empower us to forgive our abusers once and for all.

Click! God's light replaces the darkness of sin. It's just that simple!

But the Holy Spirit tends to work on a dimmer switch. From day to day (more likely year to year), he makes us a little more loving, a little more peaceful, and a little gentler than we were before. You will be constantly tempted to give up because you are still struggling with the same old stuff.

But it's not the same old stuff. Just like the grain in the field isn't ankle high like it was a month ago, your faith is not the same. We change slowly as the Spirit nudges that dimmer in Jesus' direction.

You have to wait.

The devil knows all too well what the Word can do, so one of his favorite lies is "This isn't working." Once he sees that you are not only hearing the Word but also protecting it from the thorns of worries, wealth, and wants, he starts to panic and increases his volume from whisper to shout: "This isn't working!"

But it is working. The Word might not have flipped you into an instant Jesus, but it did save you on Monday from saying that unkind thing in an email ("Do not let any unwholesome talk come out of your mouths" Ephesians 4:29). And it defended your heart after getting some concerning news from your doctor ("In all things God works for the good of those who love him" Romans 8:28). It snapped you out of the argument gridlock and softened your heart just enough to start a conversation instead of continuing the cold shoulder ("As far as it depends on you, live at peace with everyone" Romans 12:18).

The seed is up to something. You are growing because the Word is working.

The other day, I stumbled across some surprising goals I set for a year ago regarding my morning routine. Currently, I get up around 6:15, spend some time with Kim and the girls before they leave for school, and enjoy a quick breakfast before heading to the office.

But apparently that wasn't always the case.

A year ago, I had scribbled down this audacious goal: "Get up before 6:30 A.M."* Next was a related goal: "Eat breakfast every day."

Um, I thought, *I do that every day*. I don't always jump out of bed with my 6:00 A.M. alarm, but within three snooze-bar slaps, I am up and at 'em to kiss my family goodbye.

What I had forgotten, however, was that a year ago was different, filled with weekdays when Kim was out the door before my alarm even went off. I don't exactly recall when it happened, but, as the record proved, I had become a different person. I changed without noticing the change.

The seed of God's Word is like that too. You don't always notice its power, but the Spirit has staked his personal reputation on the effectiveness of the inspired Word. That seed is growing in unseen ways today that will lead to big changes tomorrow.

A Passionate Word for People Who Love Kids

I know I spoke about children earlier in this book, but since childhood is such a powerful and unrepeatable season of life, I figured it was worth a few extra words for those of us who influence the next generation in some way.

Dads and moms (and aunts and uncles and godparents and mentors and youth leaders and teachers), have you ever seen this diagram about urgency and importance?

---

* If you're an early bird like my bride, stop judging me for calling 6:30 audacious. That's early when you're up until 11:30 P.M. playing Zelda!

Urgent and Important	Not Urgent but Important
Urgent but not Important	Not Urgent and not Important

Business consultants love to guide leadership teams through this diagram, asking them to list all the company tasks that are (1) urgent and important, (2) urgent but not important, (3) not urgent but important, and (4) neither urgent nor important. As you can guess, the consultants then encourage their clients to stop doing unimportant things and focus on what truly matters for the future.

What always turns out to be the most significant challenge is prioritizing tasks that are not urgent but yet important (square 3). In the rush of Monday to Friday, when the phones are ringing and the inboxes are flooding with "reply ASAPs," it is natural to push un-urgent tasks to the indefinite future.

Why am I telling you this?

Because your kids' connection to God's Word is one of the most important yet seemingly least urgent parts of your day. Kindergarten starts at exactly 8:10 A.M., practice is from 3:15–4:30 P.M. sharp, and that diaper needed to be changed yesterday.* But Bible reading, prayer, and talking about God with your kids don't blare such red-light alarms.

The Word is a still, small voice, a quiet conversation with the Father.

So in the madness of keeping your kiddos alive, you don't get into the habit of Bible stories before bed. And no one dies. In fact, you save yourself the frustration of having to hold a two-year-old on your lap who wants to be anywhere but on your lap. So you put the seed back in the packet.

---

* If that is literally true for you, please call Child Protective Services on yourself.

The Word isn't all that urgent.

But Jesus' choice to call God's Word a *seed* should grab the attention of all of us who are blessed to be parents. If you have little ones at home, you have the greatest opportunity to plant seeds in fresh soil, and you have the most time to watch those seeds grow into the immense harvest of childlike faith. Before friends poke fun at her beliefs or wealth deceives him into working too much, you can sow truths about Jesus' love, the Father's presence, and the Spirit's power. Those first Bibles, with their drool-proof cardboard pages, and those daily prayers to our Lord will grow and blossom into beautiful things.

If waiting is a key to blessing, then the youngest souls among us have the most potential. If we can prioritize this important opportunity, we can start our kids on the path that leads to the very heart of God!

Paul wrote to young pastor Timothy, "From infancy you have known the Holy Scriptures, which are able to make you wise for salvation through faith in Christ Jesus" (2 Timothy 3:15). How did Timothy become spiritually wise enough to know that he was saved through faith in Jesus and not through his own efforts, like most Greeks believed? The Scriptures!

And how did he get connected to the Scriptures from his very infancy? Paul knows. "I am reminded of your sincere faith, which first lived in your grandmother Lois and in your mother Eunice and, I am persuaded, now lives in you also" (2 Timothy 1:5). Grandma Lois and Momma Eunice knew how important the Word was, and they started Timothy off with Jesus from day one.

So let me encourage you: Keep at it, Dad. You're on the right track, Mom. I know it's hard to see right now, but you are doing the most loving thing in the universe, namely, giving that little soul the love of the Creator of the universe. You, without a doubt, are experiencing frustration and rarely get expressions of appreciation, but the angels in heaven are cheering you on every time you fold your hands to pray, crank up the worship music at home, and read that same Bible story to your child. You can't see it yet, but the Word doesn't come back empty, and our Father will use those moments to do more than you expect or even imagine.

> Start children off on the way they should go, and even when they are old they will not turn from it.
>
> Proverbs 22:6

A Personal Word for Pastors

If you are a pastor or ministry leader, this chapter is essential for your work. When another pastor, the apostle Paul, wrote to the Corinthian church, he said, "We are co-workers in God's service; you are God's field" (1 Corinthians 3:9).

By calling this congregation a *field* and remembering that the Word is a *seed*, Paul set expectations that every minister should memorize. If these people are like a field and their souls are like soils, then your efforts with the Word will ask you to wait.

Don't expect your next sermon or that perfectly crafted email to flip the switch and make Angry Alan instantly agreeable. He needs time. Your compassion and counseling hours with Worrying Wendy might take months to bear fruit. She needs time. And I know you already had a heart-to-heart with Tone-Deaf Tom about how he comes off at church meetings, but some seeds need to be watered more than once. He needs time.

I'm not suggesting you excuse sin or let a lack of holiness slide. I am, rather, encouraging you to keep sowing, keep watering, and keep waiting until the day your church is different, when a first-time guest walks into a community that is not the same as it was six years ago, one that has grown and matured through your persistent work.

I planted the seed, Apollos watered it, but God has been making it grow. So neither the one who plants nor the one who waters is anything, but only God, who makes things grow. The one who plants and the one who waters have one purpose, and they will each be rewarded according to their own labor.

1 Corinthians 3:6–8

Keep sowing, pastor. Your labor is not in vain.

That might be easier to remember if you remember Jesus.

A Fresh Word about Jesus

How long did it take Jesus to save you?

Here are your options: (a) 6 Hours (b) 1 Weekend (c) 33 Years.

If you chose (a), I don't blame you. Jesus saved us from our sins by dying on the cross, and his time on the cross was approximately six hours, from 9 A.M. to 3 P.M. "He was delivered over to death for our sins" (Romans 4:25).

If you chose (b), I don't blame you either. Without his rising from the grave, Jesus' death on the cross could not have saved us, so the empty tomb of Easter morning seems to be the saving fruit that grew from the crucified seed on the tree. "He was delivered over to death for our sins and was raised to life for our justification" (Romans 4:25).

But the officially correct answer is (c). It took Jesus 33 years to save you. That was how long Jesus lived in perfect obedience to God's rules, loving every good thing that God loved and hating every sinful thing that God hated. Jesus didn't become our Savior once he climbed up on the cross; he was our Savior from his conception. "Today in the town of David a Savior has been born to you; he is the Messiah, the Lord" (Luke 2:11).

Why the trivia? Because it is a reminder that the best fruit the Spirit has ever produced, the very story of our salvation, didn't grow in a few hours or over a long weekend. Christianity is about the King of the cosmos, who started so small that Mary had to be told she was pregnant. And even once Jesus was conceived by the Holy Spirit and born of the virgin Mary, the world still had to wait.

> Jesus grew in wisdom and stature, and in favor with God and man.
>
> Luke 2:52

Jesus grew up, spending years—decades!—waiting for the Father's time to arrive, faithfully keeping in step with the Spirit and protecting the seed from its spiritual enemies. As a kid, he waited. As a preteen boy, he waited. When the God-man became an actual man, he waited. While others married and had children, he waited. Then, once water turned to wine and the signs of God's coming were revealed, he waited and waited and waited.

> My hour has not yet come.
>
> John 2:4

The cross was not next to the cradle, because our rescue happened through a Savior who was willing to wait.

Jesus' patience is not, however, just an example for us to follow. It is our salvation from the sin of not following his example. It is because of Jesus that our Father has his arms open, patiently waiting for his prodigal children to come home to repentance, running to embrace us and assure us that we are still his sons and daughters, turning on the grill and turning up the music so that we can celebrate in his presence (Luke 15:20–24).

You and I are far from perfectly patient. But Jesus was patient to the point of perfection. And that is really good news while we wait for him to return.

A Final Word While You Wait

If waiting is dead last on your list of superpowers, let's end this chapter with some of God's clearest and best words on the subject, assuring our hearts that the best things are worth the wait.

> I wait for the Lord, my whole being waits, and in his word I put my hope. I wait for the Lord more than watchmen wait for the morning, more than watchmen wait for the morning.
>
> Psalm 130:5–6

> Blessed are all who wait for him!
>
> Isaiah 30:18

> Blessed are those who listen to me, watching daily at my doors, waiting at my doorway.
>
> Proverbs 8:34

> Wait for the Lord; be strong and take heart and wait for the Lord.
>
> Psalm 27:14

> I say to myself, "The Lord is my portion; therefore I will wait for him."
>
> Lamentations 3:24

> Be patient, then, brothers and sisters, until the Lord's coming. See how the farmer waits for the land to yield its valuable crop, patiently waiting for the autumn and spring rains.
>
> James 5:7

Happy waiting, brothers and sisters! Our harvest is on the way!

STUDY QUESTIONS

1. What emotional expectations do you have about church and Bible reading? How long are you able to keep up your spiritual habits when you don't notice any increase in your joy or any changes in your daily life? Finally, what points from this chapter might increase your endurance?

2. Agree/Disagree—Being a Christian in a 1st-century farming culture would be easier than being a Christian in a 21st-century technological culture.

3. Do you know a pastor who seems to be discouraged? Email, in your own words, the idea from "A Personal Word for Pastors" and put courage back into his struggling soul.

4. Evaluate: If waiting is essential to blessing, then the best fruit of your faith might be yet to come.

5. Of the six passages on waiting that conclude this chapter, which one is your favorite? Why? Find a note card, copy that passage, and place it where it can remind you frequently that God's Word is worth the wait.

PART 3

YOUR POTENTIAL (REVISITED)

9

Good Soil

Still other seed fell on good soil, where it produced a crop—a hundred, sixty or thirty times what was sown. . . . The seed falling on good soil refers to someone who hears the word and understands it. This is the one who produces a crop, yielding a hundred, sixty or thirty times what was sown. . . . Others, like seed sown on good soil, hear the word, accept it, and produce a crop—some thirty, some sixty, some a hundred times what was sown. . . . But the seed on good soil stands for those with a noble and good heart, who hear the word, retain it, and by persevering produce a crop.

Matthew 13; Mark 4; Luke 8, selected verses

"You're Different."

"Do your kids notice any difference?" I asked.

I was in the presence of what I perceived to be good soil, a man who had joined our church after recently becoming a

Christian. He described his life BC (Before Christianity) and AD (After Deliverance), noting that his desires, his habits, his very life had changed.

Which made me wonder about his kids. They were old enough to remember their father before he was adopted by the Father, so I was curious if they had seen any fruit from his new faith. They had. "You're different," his daughter remarked. "Dad, at church, you write a lot," she continued.

"Well, I'm learning a lot!" This father smiled.

Stories like this are why I love the story that Jesus told. Hearing the Word is not a hobby or a habit but a holy seed that can produce a changed life. While it is tempting to read Jesus' parable and end up anxious ("So much could go wrong!"), I prefer to focus on the potential. Think of this father and the generations of faith that might come from his allegiance to Jesus!

The exponential potential is where Jesus ends this parable too. He invites us to dream about what life might look like if the Word brought back a crop "yielding a hundred, sixty or thirty times what was sown" (Matthew 13:23). Your crop might be a college experience filled with obedience. Or it might be your involvement at a church that gives insane money away to the needy in your community while refusing to water down Jesus' command to preach repentance and forgiveness of sins in his name. Or it could be the good soil that you help cultivate in your girlfriend's soul, leading her to love God, trust God, and fear God above all things.

Let's dream a bit about our potential as we look at the conclusion to Jesus' story.

The Good Soil of Your Soul

Jesus explained, "But the seed on good soil stands for those with a noble and good heart" (Luke 8:15).

A noble and good heart is a gift from God. He promised through the prophet Ezekiel, "I will give them an undivided heart and put a new spirit in them; I will remove from them their heart of stone and give them a heart of flesh" (Ezekiel 11:19). A good heart has an undivided focus on the glory of God, fixing our eyes on what makes Jesus worthy of everything we have to give.

A noble and good heart is also the prayer of God's people. This is why David begged, "Create in me a pure heart, O God, and renew a steadfast spirit within me" (Psalm 51:10). We ask God to do for us what we cannot do for ourselves, that is, to create and sustain in us a heart that is pure and not proud, persevering and not unable to deal with pain, and perceptive enough to know that nothing in this world can produce in us the kind of joy that Jesus can.

A good heart doesn't need to get its way like the people on the path. Nor does it need the world's approval like those on the rocky soil. And it refuses to worry, chase wealth, want merely temporary things, and give up on waiting.

Paul revealed the good heart that God gave him when he wrote,

> What is more, I consider everything a loss because of the sur-passing worth of knowing Christ Jesus my Lord, for whose sake I have lost all things. I consider them garbage, that I may gain Christ and be found in him, not having a righteousness of my own that comes from the law, but that which is through faith in Christ—the righteousness that comes from God on the basis of faith.
>
> Philippians 3:8–9

Compared to God, it's all garbage. As Johnny Cash said, there is nothing as satisfying as having the kingdom of God within you.

Your friends might pity you. "You could be making so much more money!" "Dude, you're seriously not doing fantasy football this year?" "You're going to church again?" But there is nothing pitiful about a heart that is tilled up, cleared out, and prepared for the seed. Give it time, and their pity might turn to envy when God makes that seed grow.

> I am the vine; you are the branches. If you remain in me and I in you, you will bear much fruit.
>
> John 15:5

How do you end up with "much fruit"? While the entire parable is a thorough answer, Jesus ends his story with five action words: *Hear. Understand. Accept. Retain. Persevere.*

Hear the Word

> But the seed on good soil stands for those with a noble and good heart, who hear the word.
>
> Luke 8:15

This is the underlying assumption of Jesus' story. Other parables are about the busyness and backward priorities that tempt us to miss hearing the Word altogether, but not this one. By God's grace, everyone in this story comes in contact with the seed.

If that's you, praise God and well done!

There are billions of people who, I assume, will not hear the Word of God today. They will rise, eat, work, eat, work, eat, relax, and sleep, but they will not hear the message about Christ. Your day, however, is different. You are reading this book, which has seeds on every other page, giving you the potential to become and do great things.

Isn't God good to us? "[God] marked out [the nations'] appointed times in history and the boundaries of their lands. God did this so that they would seek him and perhaps reach out for him and find him" (Acts 17:26–27). You and I are living in a time and place where we can hear the Word, seek the Word made flesh, and find the One who alone can satisfy our souls.

I'll ask it again—Isn't God good to us? Who are we to be so privileged to have the seed filling our worship spaces, our nightstand drawers, and the Bible apps on our phones? But here we are, surrounded by seed. Thank you, Lord!

And while I'm at it, I'll applaud your obedience and the God who is working in you to make you want to obey (Philippians 2:13). You are reading this book, even though you could be playing NBA 2K, refining your culinary skills, or catching up on email, which says something about what you value. While habits seem normal to us after time, it is no small thing to be a Bible reader, a church attender, or a sermon podcaster. The Word is there, and if the Word is indeed a seed, then those habits have holy potential.

So well done. While hearing isn't the end of this story, it is the necessary beginning.

Understand the Word

> But the seed falling on good soil refers to someone who hears the word and understands it.
>
> Matthew 13:23

Do you now understand what Jesus meant by "understand"? This isn't the ignorance you feel when the mechanic mentions your "worn out tie-rod ends."* This is the arrogance that doesn't want to hear what the Truth has to say.

But good soil wants to understand, no matter the cost or the weight of the cross. "Blessed is the one who always trembles

---

* My mechanic said that a few years ago. I just nodded as if I possessed such knowledge and said, "I concur."

before God" (Proverbs 28:14). If God wants to explain it, I want to understand it. He's God! And I'm me. Simple logic, not to mention basic humility, urges us toward understanding.

I grew up in a fairly traditional church that loved to use historic liturgies (a frequently followed service outline), classic creeds (bonus points if you can recite the Apostles' Creed from memory*), and sermon topics based off the pericope (Bible readings chosen for each week). While anything repeated can become rote and routine, there was one part of that traditional approach to worship that fit well with Jesus' story.

"The Word of the Lord."

After my childhood pastor would read the Old Testament lesson, he would say, "The Word of the Lord." Then, after reading a selection from the New Testament letters, he would repeat, "The Word of the Lord." Finally, after a few verses from one of the gospels, he would re-repeat, "The Word of the Lord."

I don't yet know the history of how that line got in there, but it seems like a good way for us to become good soil. What we just heard was the Word of the Lord. Not the word of some guy named Moses. Not the word of a decent-but-flawed Paul. Not the words the pastor up front made up. But the Word of the Lord. The Lord himself, the Holy Spirit, inspired these words, word by word. The eternal and omniscient God, the one who knows what was, what is, and what is to come, guided the prophets and apostles to write these words. When the Bible is opened, however challenging the reading might be, these words come from the Lord.

Human beings, limited by our nature and influenced by how we were nurtured, have little right to question the Lord. He

---

* And I'll give you a free copy of this book if you can do the same with the Athanasian Creed!

is not a contestant on *American Idol*, and we are not Simon Cowell. He is God. We are us.

So speak, Lord. We long to hear your voice. We want to understand your Word.

There is a young man from our church who was recently baptized into Jesus' name. He's a smart kid who locks eyes with me every time I preach, absorbs every word, and runs each point through his analytical mind. Although he didn't grow up with much Jesus, he now is trying to put down some good roots in his new Christian faith.

The other day, this new member of God's family said the perfect thing to me: "Who am I?" He had been reading some of the more challenging passages in the Bible, wrestling with their meaning and implications for his life, but then the light bulb went on—Who am I? Who am I to say this is wrong? Who am I to judge God? Who am I to tell Jesus he needs to change his mind and agree with me?

"Good soil refers to someone who hears the word and understands it." We understand the Word when we want to, and we want to when we remember who we are and, more important, who God is.

He is good. He knows better. He wants what's best.

Accept the Word

> Others, like seed sown on good soil, hear the word, accept it, and produce a crop.
>
> Mark 4:20

The word *accept* means to agree to, to follow, to surrender to, to yield. Noble and good hearts do the same with God's Word—we agree to the Word, follow the Word, surrender to the Word, and yield to the Word.

Even if those we love don't.

It is easier to accept the Word when everyone around you is applauding. If your parents have been praying for your salvation and your closest friends are the people God used to bring you to Jesus, then there is little fear in confessing your faith.

But when your parents think organized religion is a hustle, and your boyfriend was rather enjoying your previous views on sex before marriage, and your best friend is a practicing Buddhist, then it can be hard to accept the Word and everything within it.

Your baptismal waters might have been wonderful, but the hot sun of their disapproval is not.

Martin Luther felt this tension. When God used a little seed from the book of Romans to produce a reformation in the church, the German monk soon found himself pressured, accused, and even threatened. He was summoned to the Diet of Worms* in 1521, and the Holy Roman Emperor and his associates pressured Luther to recant and apologize for the things he had written since he discovered Paul's teaching about being right with God.

Martin started to sweat and asked for more time to think and to pray.

The next day, however, Martin Luther made a history-changing choice—he accepted the Word. With renewed faith, he said, "If, then, I am not convinced by proof from Holy Scripture, or by cogent reasons, if I am not satisfied by the very text I have cited, and if my judgment is not in this way brought into subjection to God's Word, I neither can nor will retract anything; for it cannot be either safe or honest for a Christian to speak against his conscience. Here I stand; I cannot do otherwise; God help me! Amen."[1]

I am bound by Scriptures. My conscience is captive to the Word of God. Amen.

---

* Which, to this day, holds the record as Worst Church Conference Name ever.

Think of the fruit that came out of that single moment, a reformation that helped countless people rely on grace and faith and the Word and Christ. Historically, however, that "crop" came out of a moment when one man didn't just hear and understand the Word but also accepted it.

Luther didn't regret it. Neither will you.

While I do not know your future, I do know that the Word will cost you something. You will lose someone's love because of Jesus, no matter how humbly you try to explain what you believe and why you believe it, and that loss will tempt you to set down your cross, turn around, and let Jesus go on without you.

But please believe that God will give you much more in return, even if that joy and peace haven't ripened just yet.

> And everyone who has left houses or brothers or sisters or father or mother or wife or children or fields for my sake will receive a hundred times as much and will inherit eternal life. But many who are first will be last, and many who are last will be first.
>
> Matthew 19:29–30

A hundred times as much? *Hmm* . . . that sounds familiar.

Retain the Word

> But the seed on good soil stands for those with a noble and good heart, who hear the word, retain it, and by persevering produce a crop.
>
> Luke 8:15

To *retain* means to maintain, preserve, or conserve, words that draw our minds back to a good garden. Although the thorns are thorny,* only that which is cared for produces a crop. *The*

---

* Fact: Late in the writing process, authors run out of good adjectives.

Message, a contemporary paraphrase of the Bible, says, "But the seed in the good earth—these are the good-hearts who seize the Word and hold on no matter what, sticking with it until there's a harvest."

Seize the Word and hold on *no matter what*.

That's a fresh way to talk about the worries of life, the deceitfulness of wealth, and wanting all the "other things" the world has to offer. The only way this Word is going to work is if we hold on to it no matter what, if we grab on to God with both hands and refuse to let him go.

When you carry groceries from your trunk and into your fridge, your hands can only handle so much. A jug of milk in this hand, a plastic bag around this wrist, and the paper bag with the canned goods on the other arm. While one trip from car to kitchen would be great, we all know that our bodies have limits.

Retaining the Word is the same. We simply don't have enough time in our limited lives to do everything for everyone. Choose A and you probably won't have time to retain B and C. In the case of Jesus' parable, choose too much of what the world is offering you, and you won't have enough time left over to hear the Word, meditate upon it, and then put it into practice.

It would be great to be the #1 volunteer at church, the top performer at work, and the one who writes a personalized birthday message to every "friend" on Facebook, but you can't fit all that in your hands while first holding on to God. God is both hefty and worthy, and putting his Word into practice is a lot to carry.

But good hearts pick up God first.

Your mind will need some time to explore the implications of Jesus' invitation, the height and width and depth of a love that invites you to come to him, lay your burdens down, and find rest for your soul. You might be able to read "It is finished" in a few seconds, but meditating on Christ's words will cost a little more time.

But the truth of the gospel is worth retaining.

I might need some space to love Kim like Christ loves his church and to be a glimpse of our Father to the kids who call me their father. Hearing the commands that God has for spouses and parents is fairly simple. But putting them into practice requires time. I might have to cut back on Zelda to help Kim with her to-do list and be a B- pastor who doesn't respond to texts ASAP if ASAP requires me to multitask during dinner with my daughters.

But a healthy and holy family is worth retaining.

You might have to stay two promotions below your capacity if you long to love people like Jesus did. It's hard to love well at 70 mph, and most of us push past the posted limit. Reconsidering your relationship with streaming TV and social media will be painful, but you just might free up your hands to reach out to the couple in your apartment hallway or be there for your sister when her marriage is barely hanging on.

But love, the greatest of God's commands, is worth retaining.

Unless you are God, you have limits. So use your limited time to do what matters most when all is said and done, hearing God's Word and having the margin to meditate upon it and put it into practice.

This past week I read the brilliant response Nehemiah gave when rebuilding the wall of Jerusalem. His critics wanted him to come down from the wall, taking a break from his God-given mission, but Nehemiah replied, "I am carrying on a great project and cannot go down. Why should the work stop while I leave it and go down to you?" (Nehemiah 6:3).

Child of God, you are carrying on a great project. While you might not have a book of the Bible named after you, the good works that God has planned for you are worthy of your priorities. Seeking God first, honoring your parents as they age, and inviting a new church member over for dinner are good works that outweigh the smaller rewards of lesser things.

Love is worth it, so retain it. Call down to competing priorities, "Why should the work stop while I leave it and go down to you?"

Persevere with the Word

> But the seed on good soil stands for those with a noble and good heart, who hear the word, retain it, and by persevering produce a crop.
>
> Luke 8:15

Persevering is another way to talk about waiting. You could call it persisting or enduring or 26.2-ing. It's taking another step when it would be much easier to give up and sit down. It's crossing mile 19 in a marathon with aching quads, believing that the finish line will make the hardest miles worth it. People who persevere stick around when the thin-skinned crowd has come and gone, because they believe that God is worthy of the wait.

A. H. Strong tells the story of a student who asked the school president if there was a shorter and faster way to finish his studies. "Oh, yes," the president replied, "but then it depends on what you want to be. When God wants to make an oak, he takes a hundred years, but when he wants to make a squash, he takes six months."[2] Robby Gallaty, in his book *Here and Now*, retells the story and then asks, "Do you want to be a squash or an oak?"[3]

God often takes a long time in forming the best things. That's true of you too.

You might be the only high school senior who cares about protecting the vice principal's reputation from the grumbling that fills the lunchroom, but you will not regret persevering. Ten years from now, when you read Jesus' words about loving your neighbor, you will remember your words and either smile or hang your head in shame. Persevere!

You might be the only single woman in your group of friends who holds to holy standards, refusing to compromise generations of faith in your family just to get a guy who makes you feel less alone in the world. When you are old and look back on your life, you will never regret seeking your Redeemer before your romantic life. Persevere!

You might be the only Republican to speak up to your Republican parents, reminding them that Jesus alone is our highest allegiance, and our unquestioned allegiance is only to him. Yes, your gentle rebuke might make things awkward, but there is great joy in knowing you have not given Caesar your soul. Persevere!

There will be rainy spring days and dry Julys, seasons when you want to give up on this yet-to-produce garden, but don't. Persevere in what you have heard, holding on to God's promises until each one is fulfilled.

> The one who calls you is faithful, and he will do it.
>
> 1 Thessalonians 5:24

He will do it. He will. Not *might* or *maybe* or *let's hope for the best.* God cannot be faithful and yet fall short of what his Word has promised.

So hear and understand, accept and retain, persevere to the end.

It will be worth it.

Holy Crop

> Others, like seed sown on good soil, hear the word, accept it, and produce a crop—some thirty, some sixty, some a hundred times what was sown.
>
> Mark 4:20

While "exponential potential" may seem like a rhyming exaggeration, I can think of no better phrase to explain Jesus' words. Some seeds bring a harvest thirty times greater than themselves. Some double that, bringing back sixty times the original seed. And some—sit down for this one—produce a crop a hundred times what was sown!

Holy crop!

If there was a stock that had the potential to increase its value a hundred times, wouldn't you invest? According to Jesus, the Word has blue-chip potential, and its heavenly CEO has a history of massive returns on small investments. Not every church service will be a "hundred-times" Sunday, but even thirty times is a lot of peace, joy, and love.

One little verse on righteousness could start a reformation in your family, just like it reformed Martin Luther's heart. You could be the first one to grasp that people get to heaven not by being good but by trusting in a good God, not by working your way there but by believing in the work of the One who came from there, not by climbing up some moral ladder but by clinging to a wooden cross.

How much fruit could come from hearing, understanding, accepting, retaining, and persevering with this single verse: "For it is by grace you have been saved, through faith—and this is not from yourselves, it is the gift of God" (Ephesians 2:8).

A single seed on justice could bring America one step closer to Amos' prayer: "But let justice roll on like a river, righteousness like a never-failing stream!" (Amos 5:24). God could use one passage to lead you down a path where thirty precious souls are saved from injustice. Maybe sixty. Maybe—God, make it so!—a hundred.

For me, it was one line on God's presence, scribbled by a guy you may never have heard of. Asaph penned, "Earth has nothing I desire besides you," the English translation of just four Hebrew words (Psalm 73:25). Yet that seed grew into an infatuation, a cover-to-cover journey through the Bible where I would become addicted to God's presence.

Who knew that one verse could bring back so much fruit?

Ahem. Jesus did.

Let his words shake small thoughts out of your mind. God's Word is a seed, and seeds have exponential potential.

Funeral Fruit

A few months back, I pitched the big idea of this book to a colleague who has a wonderfully analytical mind. In addition to some helpful feedback, he shared the story of some fruit he had just enjoyed at a funeral.

His father's best friend had just passed after a two-year battle with colon cancer at age 55. One of his dying wishes was that his funeral service be filled with classic children's praise songs, the kind that kids learn when sitting on carpet squares in the church basement.

So the organ reminded everyone of the tune and the song began:

> I am Jesus' little lamb;
> Ever glad at heart I am,
> For my Shepherd gently guides me,
> Knows my needs and well provides me,
> Loves me every day the same,
> Even calls me by my name.[4]

If you assume the deceased's friends* were too embarrassed to sing kiddie songs, you'd be wrong. Instead, diaphragms belted words off the walls of the church as grown men grew

---

* True confession—I originally wrote an apostrophe-free "the deceased friends," which turned this into an interesting sentence. Thankfully, editing is a thing!

red-eyed and tender. For many, God had planted a seed in the soil of their hearts decades ago, and just then it was bearing its biggest harvest, producing peace and joy in the face of cancer and grief.

> A farmer went out to sow his seed. . . . It came up and yielded a crop, a hundred times more than was sown.
>
> Luke 8:5, 8

STUDY QUESTIONS

1. Looking back on your personal faith journey, which biblical truths have brought back a thirty-, sixty-, or hundred-times harvest in your life? At the time, did you sense the potential of that particular part of God's Word?

2. Challenge: Interview an older Christian whose faith you respect and ask them question #1 above. What seed produced great fruit in their life? What exactly did that fruit look like? What threats did God powerfully overcome to protect that seed until it produced a crop?

3. Which of the following words do you find the hardest? *Hear. Understand. Accept. Retain. Persevere.* What

is it about you/your situation that makes that word a struggle?

4. Evaluate this statement: Christians persevere when they focus on the potential crop and not the present cost.

5. Reread the parable of the sower in its entirety in all three versions. What do you see now that you didn't see when you last read the story in chapter 2 of this book? How might your future life of faith be different from having dug so deep into Jesus' story about our souls?

6 Paul once wrote about "Christ in you" being our certain hope (Colossians 1:27). How does knowing that Christ is so near strengthen you as you seek to protect the Word? Be specific.

10

Conclusion

Whoever has ears, let them hear.

Matthew 13:9

Chuckin' Seed

On an average spring day in 2012, I made a mess in our church. The members who made up the weekly cleaning crew must have been cringing as I was preaching, because the longer I talked, the dirtier the church got.

I was preaching on the parable of the sower, and to help listeners visualize Jesus' words, I had set up a giant fish tank in the front of the church. The tank was divided into three sections—one with rocky soil, another with thorny soil, and the final with rich, brown soil. As I read through the text, I grabbed a handful of seeds from a burlap sack and sprinkled it over and around the tank. Dozens of seeds fell upon the hard tile below without a centimeter of soil, a hope, or a prayer. Others scattered amidst the rocks, got lost in the thorns, or nestled into the good ground at the edge of the tank as I explained the soils from Jesus' story.

But then I got to the application.

Refilling my hands with seeds, I looked up at the teenagers sitting in the front row and grinned. Cocking back my arm, I fired a seedy fastball in their direction, causing some to gasp and others to instinctively duck for cover.* "This is what happens every Sunday," I preached as I reached for more seed. "And this is what happens every time we sing of Jesus' love." "And this," I kept on as I reloaded, "is like Bible class or your next home devotion."

I wound up to spray another fistful of seeds when I locked eyes with a young mom sitting in the front pew, rotating her shoulders to protect the infant in her arms from my slightly aggressive sermon illustration.

That felt like the right place to stop.

But it's a good place to start my final encouragement. God is throwing seed in your direction. Every time you hear the Word, your heart has the potential to produce an exponential crop.

Don't be deceived by the smallness of the church, the dated tie of the preacher, or the normality of your morning devotion, because you are in the presence of the powerful Word of God, the message that gives new life, fresh faith, and encouragement to do the right thing for the right reason (James 1:18; Romans 10:17; 15:4).

What Combination of Soils Am I?

For it being a fairly short story, there is a lot in Jesus' words to process. For goodness' sake, you just read a 50,000-word book based off a parable that, in its longest version, is only 525 words!

---

* Because I'm a lifelong soccer player, my fastball has been clocked at nearly 4 mph, so the kids were truly terrified.

But there is depth in this message that deserves your attention, so take some time to process how you fit into each verse.

Back in college, my first religion professor encouraged our class not to see ourselves as one specific kind of soil but as an ever-shifting combination of all four soils. The hardened path might best describe someone who doesn't believe at all, but I can relate to the kind of pride that doesn't really want to understand what God's Word says to my specific situation. Likewise, the rocky soil is primarily about people who give up on God to make life easier, but what Christian hasn't withered under the pressure of peers or the desire to impress someone they like? My professor's point was that it might be more beneficial for us to ask questions such as:

What combination of soils was I this past week?

How often did pride prevent the Word from doing anything in my heart? Did I ever stay quiet when I should have spoken up just to avoid the pain of disapproval? When did I allow myself to become so busy that I didn't have much time or energy to meditate on the Word or obey its call to love others in my life? And when, by God's grace, did the Word do something beautiful, reminding me that I am forgiven and inspiring me to serve someone in love?

How did this week's combination compare to last week's?

While none of us will reach perfection this side of heaven, God calls us to grow. So has my faith progressed in the past year, giving more seeds more opportunity to produce fruit? Am I humbling myself more often when confronted by the more convicting parts of the Word? Am I sorry for sinful things that didn't bother me a year ago? Am I saying no to more money more often so that I have the space required for the Bible to bless me in even better ways? Just like the fish tank from my seed-throwing sermon contained all kinds of soils, our hearts can too.

Here's a little help to get you started, a quick summary of what we have covered so far:

Pride: How often do you want to understand God's Word? Are there any topics/teachings that make you defensive? How often do you humbly believe God is good, God knows better, and God wants what's best?

Pain: Which biblical truths do "your people" dislike? How often do you take God's side when truth causes trouble? Do you believe that he is greater than them, that his approval is greater than theirs, and that your eternity is greater than now?

Worries: How often does your worry make you busy, busy, busy? Are you ruthlessly eliminating hurry in your life so God's Word has the space it needs to grow? When was the last time you said no to something good so that you could say yes to something better?

Wealth: How often has wealth deceived you into a life that lacks rest? How might giving away riches, researching rich people, or meditating on the riches you have in Christ help you reprioritize your life?

Wanting: How often do "other things" like shows, sports, apps, and news leave you with less time than you need to hear, meditate, and apply God's Word? What better things might you gain if you abstained from lesser things?

Not Waiting: Are there any good habits, such as prayer or going to church, that you gave up on because you didn't see them working? How might remembering dimmer switches, human development, and the way seeds grow restore your trust in the power of God's Word?

This self-analysis, of course, is rather subjective. Unlike a running app, you can't spit out your progress with a few simple clicks, but it is worth our time to process our progress.

Perhaps this is where a few trusted friends can step in. Buy them a tall glass of grapefruit juice,* read the parable together, and ask them for some candid feedback based on the questions

---

* Or a good cup of coffee if they happen to be one of those weirdos who doesn't like grapefruit juice.

on the previous page. "Wounds from a friend can be trusted" (Proverbs 27:6). Their encouragement can too.

Don't fear the harder edges of the feedback you get. Don't be overwhelmed by how far you have to go. Don't live with the guilt of the things you cannot go back and change. After all, Jesus named this the parable of the sower.

Parable of the Sower?

One of the quirkier details of Jesus' parable is its title. Jesus himself labeled his story when he said, "Listen then to what the parable of the sower means" (Matthew 13:18).

The longer I studied the story, the less convinced I was that Jesus had gotten his title right. After all, the sower is barely mentioned, especially when compared to the constant repetition of "seed," "soil," and the "someone" who hears the Word.

The parable of the seed fits better, doesn't it? The parable of the soils feels more textual too. And, if you wanted to intrigue the marketing types, call it "The Seed, the Soil, and Your Soul."*

So why do you think Jesus went with the parable of the sower? Here's what I eventually concluded: because God deserves our praise. While we are thinking about the potential of sermons and songs and the threats of worries and wealth, God is at work. The One who sowed with great expectation doesn't step away, in some minor role, and hope that we protect the seed as we should.

Thankfully, God does much more than that. Much, much, much more. Although the devil would have loved for pride to snatch up every seed and for the world to wither every unpopular Word, God was at work. Even though the world offered "just

---

* Have I mentioned that pastors like alliteration? Nearly as much as I apparently enjoy footnotes about grapefruit juice.

one more" click, purchase, video, headline, and game, our Father was like a good farmer, infatuated with protecting his field.

"You are God's field," Paul taught, and "God has been making it grow" (1 Corinthians 3:9, 6).

The more I ponder the existence of any fruit in my life, the more I am stunned. Given the weakness of my flesh, the résumé of the devil, and the influence of this world, my soul should be fruitless soil.

But it's not. I'm not. Neither are you.

We are far from perfect trees who produce flawless fruit. But the fact that I don't idolize my work is a phenomenon of God's grace and worthy of on-my-knees-with-hands-stretched-high praise. Your simple belief that the Bible is God's source of glorious truth is a testament to the tenacity of God. If you give money to others, any money, especially the first chunk of your money, joyfully and generously, despite the millions of ads that lure you to live and not give, you are living proof that the Sower is a miracle worker.

If you have forgiven your dad for his flaws, God was at work.

If you didn't end up drunk, high, or out of control last weekend, God was at work.

If you turned the other cheek or stood up for someone who wasn't there to defend themselves, God was at work.

If you believed that, despite your sins, there is still a place for you in heaven, God was at work.

If you were diagnosed with cancer but trusted that death couldn't separate you from Jesus' love, God was at work.

When I stand by my garden and pluck a tomato, I look around and marvel. How many storms, winds, bugs, and bunnies could have—should have!—prevented this fruit from being here? But here it is, protected by my small efforts and preserved by God's enormous grace.

Martin Luther, who should have been dead long before he changed the church, wrote:

> Blest be the Lord, who foiled their threat
> That they could not devour us.
> Our souls, like birds, escaped their net;
> They could not overpow'r us.
> The snare is broken—we are free!
> Our helper and our strength is he
> Who made the earth and heavens.[1]

If it wasn't for the Sower, the seed wouldn't have survived. If it wasn't for God, your faith wouldn't have either.

So praise God for fruit! For all fruit and any fruit, for every moment of joy in the Lord and every act of love done in his name, for self-control against temptation and patience when things didn't go our way. Lord, we thank you for making your Word grow. We heard and tried to hang on to Scripture, but you deserve your name in the title of our story because every good and perfect gift, fruit included, is from above.

And while our eyes are fixed on heaven, let's take the opportunity to praise the Savior who offers hope to every proud, weak, and worried soul who reads this parable with regret. Perhaps you have processed the great percentage of words that didn't find good soil in your heart, and you realize that there is no way to go back and no way to make it up to God.

If so, join me in praising God for the fruit of his Son. Jesus, the Word made flesh, was the perfect seed from heaven. Although the devil tempted him with pride and the world made his obedience painful, Jesus didn't wither. Even when he could have worried about his reputation, traded his mission for the wealth of the world, and wanted comfort more than his cross, Jesus refused to let anything stop him from producing the fruit of salvation. And then he waited until the work was done and the fruit of forgiveness was ripe and ready to enjoy.

"There is now no condemnation for those who are in Christ Jesus" (Romans 8:1). None. Right now. So shake off the regret and the self-loathing. Through faith in Jesus, you are God's field, good soil that has the Sower's full attention. This year is another season where he will sow seed and do everything in his power to help it, and you, produce good fruit.

This Book (Kind of) Changed Me

Back in the introduction, I mentioned that ten months have passed between my first draft of this book and this second edition, a long enough gap for me to personally test the concepts that I have been claiming have fruit-producing power. But did anything actually change for me?

The candid answer is—kind of. As I type this section, which obviously didn't exist in the first draft, I have seen some undeniable changes in my life as well as some regrettable behaviors that didn't change at all.

For example, after gushing in this book about my late-night Zelda quests, I put the controller down cold turkey. Seriously. After completing 90% of the game, I just stopped. With every intention to make Ganon, the final boss, taste the sharpened edge of the Master Sword and then to start my venture into the never-ending world of FIFA 21, I simply walked away.*

What changed? It dawned on me that video games were "other things" that were getting in the way of the things that mattered more to me. Like crawling into bed at the same time as my wife in order to decompress, catch up on the day, and pray about the week ahead. Or like reading good books while my family slept to help me be a better husband, better father, and better follower of Jesus. Or like sleeping a solid eight hours so I could start the next day with an open Bible and an alert brain instead of rushing my quiet time before I rushed out the door.

* Kim is deeply saddened that I can no longer regale her with regular tales of my digital bravery. #sarcasticfootnote

I'm not hating on Zelda or FIFA or anyone who spends their free time in front of a screen. I am saying that thinking critically about "other things" changed me. In other words, this book changed me, because Jesus' parable changed me.

Kind of. I have to admit that other things barely changed. My prayer life, for example, is still as sporadic as it used to be. I do pray each day, but I am far from a prayer warrior. I am more like a prayer intern. On his first day. Maybe.

Why haven't I changed? About a year ago, I preached an entire sermon series called *Pray Like a Pro*, a series that turned into a book to improve your prayer life, which turned into several radio/podcast interviews where I got to talk about improving your prayer life. Given all the Word that I heard/read/shared, why didn't my prayer life improve?

Thinking back on the threats in Jesus' parable is a helpful way to explain what happened:

Pride—Did I not want to understand the power and priority of prayer? I don't think so.

Pain—Did my unbelieving loved ones threaten to persecute me if I prayed more? Definitely not.

Worries—Was I worried that more time in prayer would jeopardize something I needed more time for? Not that I can recall.

Wealth—Was I so busy making money that I ran out of time to pray? Nope.

Wanting—Did I desire so many "other things" that my life was too cluttered for prayer? *Hmm*. That hits home.

Not Waiting—Is my stagnated prayer life due to impatience? Am I losing my fire for prayer because I don't see immediate answers from God? That's a possibility too.

I realized that my primary problems with prayer are my beliefs and behaviors. My faulty belief, previously unspoken, is that my prayers must not be working because I don't see many results after I pray (threat #6). As a result, I fill up my work schedule and my free time with "other things" instead of dedicated times of prayer (threat #5). The hard facts show that I make time for books, podcasts, scrolling the news, or jumping on social media every day, but I don't do the same with prayer.

As agonizing as this is to confess in print, it reminds me of the brilliance of Jesus' story. Real change happens when we take his words to heart. And real potential is missed when we don't.

Thankfully, there is grace for me. Even as I type these words, remembering my sin, Jesus is remembering my sins no more (Jeremiah 31:34). He isn't thinking of your sins either. God has a new covenant with you, an agreement that your failures are forgiven by the blood of Jesus and, therefore, are no longer on your Father's mind (Hebrews 10:16–18).

And there is grace upon grace to help us change, to help us believe that God's Word is worth it, however humbling, offensive, or challenging it might be in the moment. God truly is good, and he only wants what is best.

For me. For you. For us all.

100 Times What Was Sown

God must have known that I needed to see the exponential potential of his Word because, as I sat down to write this book, Mike walked into my office.

A few weeks earlier, during a sermon series on gratitude, I gave our church family a challenge to literally count their blessings. The exact wording from my sermon was, "This week, I want you to count yourself to sleep. Try to count all the good things that happened that day, the big ones and the small ones. Do an A to Z list if you want. The Apple and Bagel and Coffee for breakfast, your Dog, whatever. Train your soul to see God's goodness, because God is good."

Later that night, Mike, a 67-year-old, every-Sunday member of our church, emailed me. "Come up with 26 good gifts, A to Z? I'm pretty sure I can come up with 2,600 things."

"I dare you," I dared him, assuming that no man in his right mind would be able to list blessings that nearly equaled the number of souls saved on the day of Pentecost.

But I had forgotten that seeds have exponential potential. Two hours after my official dare, Mike emailed back. "I'm at 128 and still in the Cs."

For the next eight Sundays, this persistent Christian began every conversation in the church lobby with a number and a letter, updating me on the overall blessing count and how far through the alphabet he had gotten. Before long, triple-digit blessings crossed the millennium mark; 1,000 grew to 1,500, 1,500 to 2,000. Then, despite the difficulties of the Qs and Xs, Mike reached 2,500. Finally, an email showed up with the subject line "10, 9, 8 . . ."

That Friday, Mike scheduled a time to talk face-to-face, and in his hands he held a binder that I won't throw out for the rest of my life. Because there, on 37 separate pages, in tiny type, Mike had listed 2,600 different ways that our Father in heaven had blessed him.

"This changed my life," Mike shared.

What didn't hit me as I first paged through Mike's binder was the math. On the very Friday that I began writing this book about the potential of the Word, a man with good soil in his soul brought back a tremendous harvest.

"List 26 blessings," I challenged.

"Here are 2,600," he responded.

If my math is right, Mike brought back one hundred times what was sown.

That's what the Word can do.

That's your exponential potential.

Because what's big starts small.

Listen! A farmer went out to sow his seed. . . . Whoever has ears to hear, let them hear.

Mark 4:3, 9

ACKNOWLEDGMENTS

Mom, you took me to church every Sunday, even when I pretended to be sick or sleeping. You planted a seed in the stubborn soil of my heart, where God, somehow, made it grow. Thank you. And I'm sorry for punching you in the head that one day in the car.

Dad, seeing you in church each Sunday is an answer to hundreds of my prayers. I also appreciate your exposing my daughters to cable shows about catching tuna and solving homicides. They are well-rounded humans because of you.

Chris, my older brother, since you have made it clear to our family that books are overrated, I won't assume that you'll read this. But just in case this book gets turned into a movie starring Chuck Norris and Candace Cameron Bure, please know that I enjoy every time we are in the same room.

Kim, you are good soil. Most people know that after spending time with you, but I get to see that up close each day. Not many find a wife of noble character, but, by God's grace, I have. Also, would you be willing to get a second job so we could buy a $10,000 massage chair?

Brooklyn, you changed my world when you were born. Watching you mature into an intelligent and organized young woman of God brings me great joy. You are so much like your mother, which is one of the highest compliments I could ever give you. Plus, you like Justin Bieber, which proves you are a woman of noble character.

Maya, you are my little hugger and our family's greatest drummer. When I think of kindness, compassion, gentleness, love, and a "You First!" heart, I think of you and all the daily ways that you seek to serve the people God puts in your life. Thank you for interrupting our busy lives with "Wait! Hugs!" every single day.

LeBron James, if you ever want to hang out and dunk some tennis balls, let me know. Except on Sundays. I'm busy on Sundays.

Andy McGuire, you are the perfect blend of practical wisdom and personal encouragement. Thank you for helping me understand the process of publishing and for inspiring me with the right words at the right time. I thank God for you.

Ellen McAuley, you read this book and offered ideas to make it better. You did, and for that I am grateful. Also, thank you for catching more than 2,000 of my grammatical errors! I feel like there should be special seats at heaven's feast for people who do what you do.

922Ministries colleagues, I wouldn't have time to write without your partnership in the gospel. Thank you for all you do to make our church a beautiful place that is full of grace and truth for all kinds of people.

Jeno Paulucci, I know you died over a decade ago, but thank you for inventing pizza rolls. I may not have survived my teenage years without bulk-sized bags of your frozen culinary delights.

Jason Jaspersen, I will never read the parable of the sower again without thinking of your insightful angle on each of the soils. The glaring bird is my favorite (and I have lots of favorites).

Bethany Vredeveld, I couldn't draw a stick figure without it having a serious case of scoliosis, so thank you for using your strengths for others.

Charles V, I realize you died a half millennium ago, but what were you thinking with the "Diet of Worms" branding campaign? Did ancient emperors not have PR departments?

Time of Grace team, I am aware that you being listed after a dead politician and the guy who invented pizza rolls may seem insensitive, but I am truly blessed to work with you. For your ideas, your edits, your feedback, and, especially, your faith, thank you. Let's keep connecting souls to GOD!

GOD, you are worthy of all glory and honor and praise. May the thought of you never get old, no matter how many books we read about you or how many songs we sing to you.

NOTES

Chapter 4 Pain

1. Paul L. Maier, *Eusebius: The Church History* (Grand Rapids, MI: Kregel, 2007), 133.

2. Brett McCracken, "From Gay to Gospel: The Fascinating Story of Becket Cook," The Gospel Coalition, August 23, 2019, www.thegospelcoalition.org /article/gay-gospel-becket-cook.

3. Brett McCracken, "From Gay to Gospel."

Chapter 5 Worries

1. David Murray, *Reset* (Wheaton, IL: Crossway, 2017), 54.

2. Sissy Goff, *Raising Worry-Free Girls* (Minneapolis, MN: Bethany House), 100.

3. Carey Nieuwhof, *Didn't See It Coming* (Colorado Springs: Waterbrook, 2018), 84–85.

4. Bernard of Clairvaux, "O Sacred Head, Now Wounded," https://mlc -wels.edu/publications/wednesday-2021.

Chapter 6 Wealth

1. Arthur A. Just Jr., *Luke 1:1–9:50 Concordia Commentary* (St. Louis, MO: Concordia Publishing, 1997), 350.

2. Philip Yancey, *Vanishing Grace* (Grand Rapids, MI: Zondervan, 2014), 154.

3. Jean Twenge, *Generation Me* (New York: Free Press, 2006), 102.

Chapter 7 Wanting

1. Gregory Thornbury, *Why Should the Devil Have All the Good Music?* (New York: Convergent, 2018), 75.

2. Scott Sauls, *From Weakness to Strength* (Colorado Springs: David C. Cook, 2017), 122.

Chapter 9 Good Soil

1. Martin Luther's Speech at the Imperial Diet in Worms (18 April 1521), www.sjsu.edu/people/james.lindahl/courses/Hum1B/s3/Luther-Speech -Worms-1521.pdf.

2. Miles J. Stanford, *The Complete Green Letters* (Grand Rapids, MI: Zondervan, 1983), 6–7.

3. Robby Gallaty, *Here and Now* (Nashville: B&H, 2019), 179.

4. Henriette Louise von Hayn, trans. William Fleming Stevenson, "I Am Jesus' Little Lamb," public domain.

Chapter 10 Conclusion

1. Martin Luther, "If God Had Not Been on Our Side," stanza 3, public domain.

ABOUT THE AUTHOR

Mike Novotny pours his Jesus-based joy into his ministry as a pastor at The CORE (Appleton, Wisconsin) and as the lead speaker for Time of Grace, a global media ministry that connects people to God through television, print, and digital resources. Unafraid to bring grace and truth to the toughest topics of our time, he has written numerous books, including *3 Words That Will Change Your Life*, *Gay & God*, *How to Heal*, *Sexpectations*, and *No Fear Year*. Mike lives with his wife, Kim, and their two daughters, Brooklyn and Maya; runs long distances; and plays soccer with other middle-aged men whose best days are long behind them. Learn more at timeofgrace.org.

More from Mike Novotny

One short sentence can change your life: God is here. This book will help you move from just enjoying the good *moments* in life to worshiping the God who is right here, right now. It will allow you to shake off the shame of sin and see yourself as God does. Learn how to recognize God's impact on your life and find the joy he's been waiting to give you!

3 Words That Will Change Your Life

BETHANY HOUSE

Stay up to date on your favorite books and authors with our free e-newsletters. Sign up today at bethanyhouse.com.

 facebook.com/BHPnonfiction

 @bethany_house

 @bethany_house_nonfiction